Christmas

with Southern Living® 1994

By Vicki L. Ingham
and Dondra G. Parham
with the *Southern Living* Test Kitchens Staff

Oxmoor
House®

©1994 by Oxmoor House, Inc.
Book Division of Southern Progress Corporation
P.O. Box 2463, Birmingham, Alabama 35201

Southern Living® is a federally registered trademark belonging
to Southern Living, Inc.

Library of Congress Catalog Card Number: 84-63032
ISBN: 0-8487-1190-4
ISSN: 0747-7791
Manufactured in the United States of America
First Printing

Editor-in-Chief: Nancy Fitzpatrick
Senior Homes Editor: Mary Kay Culpepper
Senior Editor, Editorial Services: Olivia Kindig Wells
Art Director: James Boone

Christmas with Southern Living 1994

Editor: Vicki L. Ingham
Assistant Editor: Dondra G. Parham
Recipe Editor: Kaye Mabry Adams, *Southern Living* magazine
Southern Living Test Kitchens Director: Patty Vann
Southern Living Test Kitchens Staff: Jane Cairns,
Julia Dowling, Judy Feagin, Diane Hogan, Peggy Smith
Editorial Assistants: Rebecca C. Fitzgerald,
Jennifer K. Mathews, Karen Brechin
Copy Editor: L. Amanda Owens
Copy Assistant: Leslee Rester Johnson
Designer: Carol Middleton
Senior Photographer: John O'Hagan
Photostylist: Katie Stoddard
Associate Production Manager: Theresa L. Beste
Production Assistant: Marianne Jordan
Illustrations: Robin Richeson
Patterns: Barbara Ball

Contents

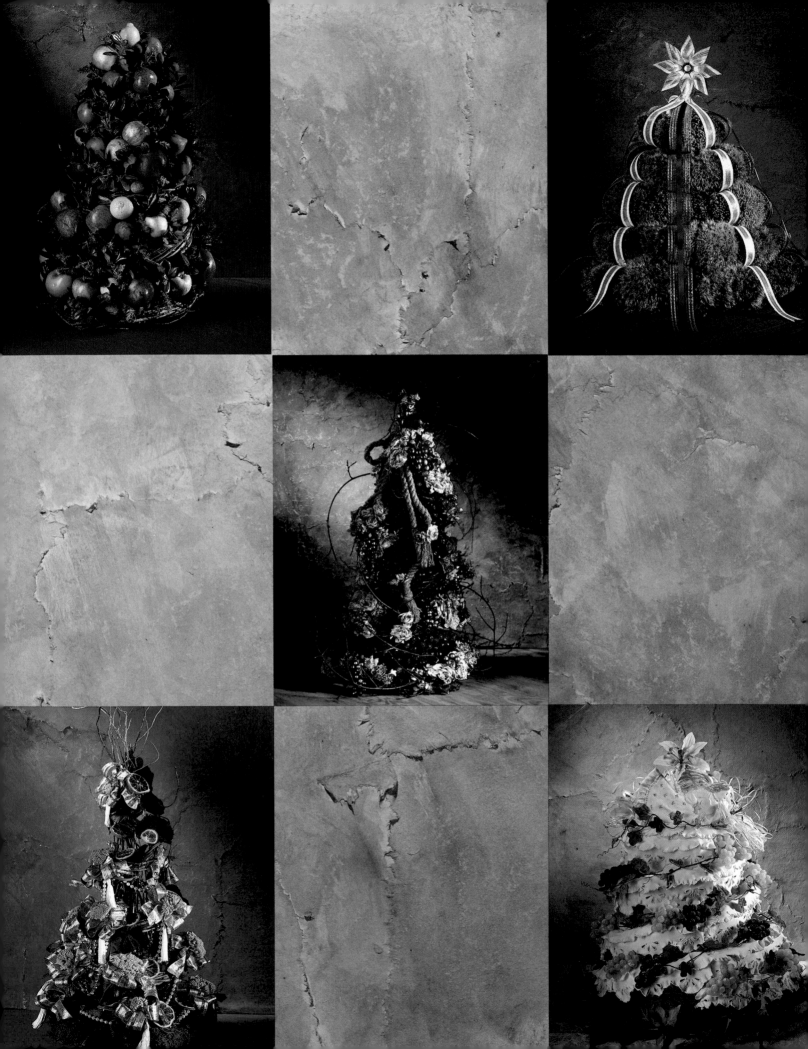

Introduction

Whether it's a floor-to-ceiling Fraser fir or a cedar cut from the roadside, the message is the same: when the Christmas tree is up, the holidays are here.

Trees small enough to fit on a tabletop let you spread that message throughout the house. There are lots of ways to make tabletop trees, but the ones you see here are unusual in that they start with a grapevine spiral. You may have seen these in crafts stores or flower shops – before they're uncoiled, they look like fat vine wreaths.

We asked five designers to take this familiar item and turn it into something spectacular. Each designer received a suggested theme and he or she took it from there. Fruit and greenery harmonize with the decorations at Tryon Palace. Tassels and pearls reflect the current influence that home decorating and fashion accessories have on crafting. Moss answers today's trend toward natural materials. A floral designer's idea for using hazelnuts and bouquets of dried roses produces an elegant, baroque holiday display. And a confectionary fantasy seems the perfect introduction to "Celebrations from the Kitchen." Meet the designers and learn how to make the trees, beginning on page 70.

What surprised and pleased us most about these trees was the way each person interpreted the assignment in his or her own distinctive and unpredictable fashion. It's a valuable reminder of how the creative process works: one idea sparks another; you take an idea and make it your own.

That's what we hope you'll do with this edition of *Christmas with Southern Living*. We've included more step-by-step photographs and illustrations than ever before to help you duplicate the projects and decorations. But you'll also find inspiration for still more ways to create a centerpiece, display a collection, or trim a mantel. Put your own spin on it, and the results will be uniquely yours.

At Christmas, there's a special zest in everything you do – baking, crafting, planning parties, and decorating your home – because it's all part of celebrating the season with joy. We hope that in the pages that follow, you'll find lots of ideas that will help you make your holidays the happiest ever!

The Editors

Christmas in the South

Crowned with Greenery, Jeweled with Fruit

Tryon Palace offers glorious Christmas decorating ideas and inspiration.

During the Christmas season, candles light the path to Tryon Palace in New Bern, North Carolina, and elaborate constructions of fruit and greenery embellish the neoclassical architecture. Visitors expect the holiday decorations to be as elegant as the building, and they're not disappointed.

Assistant Horticulturist Susan Ferguson works with professional designers Lynn James, Alan Toler, and Patricia Dixon to devise decorations that combine traditional materials with new ones for a fresh, sophisticated look. For *Christmas with Southern Living* readers, Susan used some of these elements to design the wreath shown on page 12.

The decorations at the Palace are large-scale to suit the proportions of the building, but Susan says that you can apply the ideas and techniques at home, too. The semicircular arrangement on the porch pediment, for example, "is just a really large badge," says Susan. You can easily scale it to fit over your own door or make several small ones to mount over your windows. "Making them is more fun to do with a group," says Susan,

Tryon Palace, built in 1770 as the seat of royal government in North Carolina, is open daily. At Christmas, candlelight tours bring 18th-century celebrations to life, with music, dance, decorations, and games.

"so you might think about getting together with your neighbors for a day of decorating and have everyone help each other make the arrangements and hang them." To learn how to construct the pediment badge, see page 14.

The fruit-and-flower arrangements at the Palace are more lavish than anything Governor Tryon and his wife would have created in 1770, when the original Palace was completed. Rather, they reflect the spirit of the Colonial Revival style of the 1930s. Coinciding with the restoration of Colonial Williamsburg, the style influenced everything from residential architecture to furniture reproductions to flower arranging. Floral designers charged with decorating early house museums drew inspiration from the fruit and floral motifs in baroque and rococo engravings, overmantel carvings, and picture frames, and interpreted them with real fruits, flowers, and ribbons.

Today, most house museums take a stricter approach, emphasizing documentation and historical accuracy, but Susan Ferguson still has a freer hand at the Palace. This is partly because of popular demand and partly because the Palace that visitors see today was actually built from 1952 to 1959. The original building, designed by English architect John Hawkes, burned to the ground in 1798, when sparks from a servant's torch ignited

The garland for the main staircase is made from separate ropes of pine and boxwood twisted together. To festoon your own stair this way, allow one and one-half to two times the length of the stair rail for each swag or loop.

hay stored in the basement. The Palace was reconstructed 160 years later on the original foundations and following the original plans.

Tryon Palace is the centerpiece of a 14-acre museum and garden complex, which includes four historic house museums and the New Bern Academy. These range in date from the 1780s to the early 19th century and, for the holidays, are decorated authentically according to each period. As Administrator Kay Williams explains, "Our historic sites show what happens to Christmas celebrations over time. So at each building, you can experience a different period from the past."

Tryon Palace Historic Sites and Gardens are open daily for tours. On five evenings, there are candlelight tours featuring costumed enactors who sing carols, dance to the music of a harpsichord, play cards, cook, and give visitors a glimpse of how Christmas might have been celebrated in our nation's early years.

Visiting Tryon Palace Historic Sites and Gardens

How to get there: Take U.S. 70 from Raleigh to New Bern or U.S. 17 from Wilmington.

Where to stay: There are several charming bed-and-breakfasts, as well as major motels. For a list, call the Craven County Visitors Bureau, 919-637-9400 or 800-437-5767.

For Christmas 1994 tour information: Call Tryon Palace, 800-767-1560. Reservations for either daytime or evening tours aren't necessary for individuals, but groups of 20 or more can receive a discount on admission prices if arrangements are made in advance. To learn how to make some of the Palace's holiday decorations, you can attend a one-day workshop. The first session is usually held on a Saturday in mid-November. Admission is with a $4 Gardens tour ticket or a $10 advance Christmas tour ticket. The second workshop is usually on a Wednesday in mid-December. Admission is by purchase of a Christmas tour ticket.

What else to see: New Bern is the state's second oldest town and boasts more than 200 buildings on the National Register of Historic Places. For walking tour maps, call the Visitors Bureau.

Food displays at the Palace change every year to reflect new research. The fruit pyramids at the corners were a typical decorative dessert in the 18th century.

How to Make a Tryon Palace Wreath

Susan Ferguson, one of the horticulturists at Tryon Palace, adds color and texture with dyed glycerinized leaves and baby's breath.

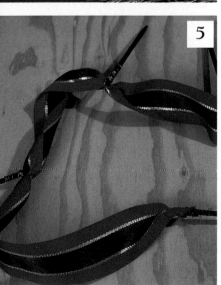

1. Start with a standard straw wreath form tightly wrapped with plastic Wreath Wrap. For a sturdy hanger, either push wire through the straw and twist it into a loop or secure a length of twine with a fern pin.

2. Assemble a cluster of 2- to 4-inch-long sprigs of fir, boxwood, and pine. Secure to the inside edge of the wreath form with a fern pin. Repeat to cover both inside and outside edges of the form and then the front, being careful to point all clusters in the same direction. Each succeeding cluster should cover the pin and stems of the preceding cluster.

3. For contrasting texture, add glycerinized or silk oak leaves. Wire them to florist's picks and then wrap stem and pick with florist's stem wrap to cover the wire. With the top of the wreath pointing away from you, insert the oak leaves along the sides and front, varying the angles.

4. For color, clip nandina berries into small sprigs, wire to florist's picks, and insert around the front and inner edge of the wreath. Repeat with baby's breath for a bright accent.

5. Cut a length of ribbon about the circumference of the wreath. At 3- to 4-inch intervals, pinch the ribbon and wrap it with the wire on the florist's pick.

6. Use a fern pin to secure a bow to the top of the wreath. Add the ribbon, angling the picks to create a more interesting line around the front of the wreath.

Tips from Tryon Palace
for Making a Pediment Badge

Preparing the Base

Cut heavy-duty, 2-inch-thick Styrofoam to fit your pediment. Styrofoam of this thickness comes in 12-inch by 36-inch or 24-inch by 36-inch sheets. If you need a larger base, glue sheets together using white craft glue or low-temperature hot glue. To hold the sheets together until the glue dries, insert toothpicks or florist's picks into the edges before gluing. To make cutting easier, use a serrated knife and wax the blade by drawing it through an old candle several times.

1. The badge will hang from a nail in the woodwork. To make the hanger, about one-third of the distance from the top of the base, push heavy florist's wire through the Styrofoam from front to back. Bring it back to the front, leaving enough wire on the back to form the hanger. Insert a dowel between the wire and the Styrofoam on the front and back of the base.

2. On the back, twist the wire tightly so that it holds the dowel firmly against the base. Leave a loop for hanging. On the front, twist the wires over the dowel, then bend the ends and push them into the Styrofoam. For a large badge, use two hangers, evenly spaced across the top third of the badge.

Securing the Pineapples

You can either use whole pineapples or cut them in half and seal the cut side with melted paraffin.

1. Center the first pineapple on the base with the leaves near the top. Push dowels into the Styrofoam, forming a shelf on which the bottom of the pineapple will rest.

To secure the pineapple to the base, wire it below the leaves by pushing heavy florist's wire through the Styrofoam and twisting tightly on the back. Push the ends of the wire into the Styrofoam.

2. Angle a pineapple on each side of the center pineapple, securing in the same way with wire and dowels. Finally, "nail" each pineapple to the Styrofoam with florist's picks pushed through the side of the fruit and into the Styrofoam.

Adding Fruits and Greenery

Using fern pins or pieces of florist's wire bent into a hairpin shape, attach magnolia leaves around the edges of the base. Referring to the photograph, fill in around the pineapples with oranges, apples, and lemons, securing them with florist's picks. If necessary, tuck bits of greenery among the fruit to hide the Styrofoam.

After you hang the badge, add magnolia branches around the edges to hide the sides and to loosen and soften the outline of the shape.

This pediment decoration is just a large badge on a Styrofoam base. The secret to hanging it securely is to insert a 2-inch-long, ¹/₄-inch-diameter dowel between the base and the hanging wire. (See illustrations at left.)

It's a Cowboy Christmas in Oklahoma

**This family rounds up
Old West memorabilia for
holiday decorations.**

Decorations of apples and box-wood may be fine for a house in Virginia, but Vicky and Don Smith want something more distinctively regional for their farm home in Luther, Oklahoma. The log house, which they designed themselves, is filled with Navajo blankets, cowboy art, and one-of-a-kind furnishings by New West Design. So when it's time to decorate for the holidays, what could be more appropriate than a western theme?

The Smiths' decorations are both creative and witty. A cowboy hat tops the tall cedar tree that was cut from the pasture. Stiff rope winds through the branches as garland. Real horseshoes (made of lightweight aluminum

Vicky and Don Smith and their daughter, Megan, gather in front of the fireplace. Instead of stockings, Vicky hangs cowboy boots for Santa to fill.

Right: It's a family tradition to cut a cedar from the pasture and bring it in for decorating. In keeping with the western theme, it wears rope for a garland and a cowboy hat for a topper.

Beneath a tree decorated with bandannas, cowboy hats, and ornaments with a western motif, Vicky displays a collection of old toys, spurs, books, and chaps. Gifts are wrapped in western-print paper, tied with twine, and topped with cowboy and Indian toys.

for racehorses) hang from the branches, along with bandannas, silver conchos, leather stars, and an assortment of cowboy and Indian ornaments. Instead of stockings, real cowboy boots hang from the mantel, and a barbed-wire wreath rests on the mantel shelf.

Vicky has been collecting Old West memorabilia for years, scouring flea markets for anything with cowboy, Indian, or western motifs: painted-tin Monterey ware, tablecloths, cutlery, and even vintage pajamas, which daughter Megan enjoys wearing at the farm.

Vicky can't really explain why it appeals to her so much, except that it evokes in a lighthearted way her childhood on an Oklahoma farm. "We always worked the cattle the old way," she says, "and on a farm, everybody works together. We all had our jobs to do." She describes her father as "being like the John Wayne cowboy. He never has owned a pair of shoes – he always wears boots and a cowboy hat."

The weekend and holiday retreat she and Don have created for themselves and their three children amazes their friends. "People come over and say it's neat, it looks just like Oklahoma," says Vicky.

Christmas breakfast is served on painted-tin plates, called Monterey ware, that Vicky picked up at flea markets. The 1940s tablecloth and the vintage sugar-and-cream set are flea market finds, too. The chairs are by New West Design.

Even if a Cowboy Christmas doesn't suit the style of your interiors, it might be just the thing for a child's room or for a themed tree in the den. Here are some ways to bring the look home. • Buy inexpensive bandannas or make your own from red bandanna fabric; fold and roll each one into a tube, knot it in the middle, and drape or tie it over a tree branch. • Tie ribbon or thread to inexpensive cowboy toys and use them as ornaments. • Use stiff roping as garland. • Cut craft leather into star shapes and embellish with rawhide thongs. • Purchase conchos from a crafts shop and tie on feathers or colorful strips of rawhide. • Wrap packages in plain brown paper and twine and tie on a cowboy toy. Or look for wrapping paper in a Navajo-blanket pattern. • Make our Pint-size Piñatas on page 101 and use them as package toppers and ornaments.

The Herndon Home

An African-American Family's Gift to Atlanta

At Christmas, the Herndon Home in northwest Atlanta offers a lively combination of festive decorations, family history, and a celebration of African-American culture. Completed in 1910, the house was designed and built by Alonzo and Adrienne Herndon, prominent members of the city's black elite. Their only son, Norris, inherited the house and added to its collections of antiques. Today, the Herndon Home is both a monument to this family's achievements and a living cultural institution.

Born into slavery in 1858, Alonzo Herndon spent most of his youth doing farm labor in Walton County, east of Atlanta. In 1882, he moved to Atlanta and signed on as a journeyman barber at a shop on Marietta Street. Six months later, he became a partner and over the next 45 years opened or operated at least eight other shops. In time, he also bought several insurance companies and organized them into the Atlanta Mutual Insurance Association, now known as Atlanta Life Insurance Company.

In 1893, Alonzo married Adrienne McNeil of Savannah. A graduate of the Atlanta University Normal School, she became director of the university's department of elocution and dramatics. In 1897, she gave birth to Norris, the couple's only child.

In 1900, Adrienne and Alonzo traveled through Europe. They must have been fascinated by the architecture they saw because when they began building a home near Atlanta University in 1908, they drew on their memories to create a fashionably eclectic structure that combined a variety of historical styles wrapped in a beaux arts exterior. Everything from brickmaking to woodworking was carried out by skilled black craftsmen.

Norris earned an M.B.A. from Harvard University in 1921. When Alonzo died six years later, Norris succeeded him as president of Atlanta Life Insurance Company. Both men gave generously to educational and community causes. In addition, Norris collected art, and today the Herndon Home displays his Roman glass, Greek vases, antique furniture, and Buddhist and Christian statuary.

Adrienne and Alonzo Herndon and son, Norris, in 1910. Courtesy of The Herndon Foundation.

The Herndon residence, completed in 1910, is open for tours Tuesday through Saturday. Admission is free, but large groups should make reservations.

Toys from Norris's childhood surround the tree in the upstairs sitting room. Garlands of popcorn and cranberries and a paper bell near the top recall the way the family decorated its Christmas tree.

Restored in 1982, the residence is listed on the National Register of Historic Places. It is open to the public and offers a variety of educational programs, exhibitions, and special events. At Christmas, black-owned businesses and garden clubs contribute time and materials to decorate the house. In addition to traditional arrangements of greenery and flowers, decorations feature African motifs: a tree in the entry hall is decked with masks and images drawn from the rich symbolic vocabulary of Adinkra cloth made in Ghana. On the dining room buffet, vegetables and fruits, candles, and sculpture form the Kwanzaa display. Observed from December 26 to January 1, Kwanzaa celebrates African-American heritage and culture. The Herndon Home, with its tradition of commitment to family and community, is the ideal host for this ceremony.

Visiting the Herndon Home

How to get there: From Martin Luther King, Jr. Drive, turn north on Vine Street and east on University Place. The best way to reach Martin Luther King, Jr. Drive depends on how you're approaching the city. Call the Herndon Home for directions.

For information about Christmas and Kwanzaa activities: Call 404-581-9813. The Herndon Home is open for tours Tuesday through Saturday, 10 a.m. to 4 p.m. Admission is free, and groups need reservations.

A Fruit Pyramid from the Herndon Home

Charlotte Barclay of Barclay's Flowers and Gifts created the centerpiece for the Herndon Home dining room. What makes it distinctive is the way she stacked fruits to create a layering of color and shape – a kumquat atop a tangerine, for example, or a cranberry skewered with a hat pin to an orange. Pink velvet bows pick up the color of the goblets and give the pyramid a Victorian look.

wrap and taping to a florist's pick. Insert clusters around the base of the cone.

Attach heavier fruits with florist's picks, placing them near the bottom of the cone. Lemons and limes can be secured with toothpicks.

Stack smaller fruits, such as kumquats and cranberries, on top of larger fruits, securing with pearl-tipped hat pins.

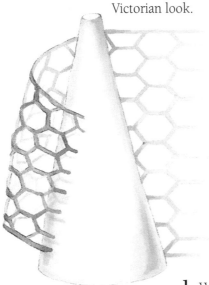

1. Wrap a Styrofoam cone with chicken wire. Insert arborvitae, cedar, or other fine-textured evergreen sprigs wired to florist's picks.

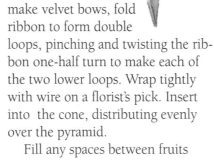

2. Assemble magnolia leaves into clusters by taping stems together with florist's stem

3. To make velvet bows, fold ribbon to form double loops, pinching and twisting the ribbon one-half turn to make each of the two lower loops. Wrap tightly with wire on a florist's pick. Insert into the cone, distributing evenly over the pyramid.

Fill any spaces between fruits with moss to cover the Styrofoam.

A lace tablecloth, Spode china, and goblets that Norris bought in Venice re-create the way the dining table looked when Norris entertained friends in the 1950s.

Holiday Traditions

Twice the Party, Twice the Fun

Call on your friends to get things done!

Dean Brunton loves to pull off a party. That's the first thing this 34-year-old bachelor told us about himself. "My love of entertaining was passed to me from my parents," says Dean. "I remember Dad would call Mom at three o'clock to say he was bringing home dinner guests. He could do that, because Mom is a great entertainer."

For the holidays, Dean hosts two parties at his home in Atlanta, Georgia. One is a huge black-tie affair. The menu highlights include caviar and champagne, raspberry-chocolate truffles, Grand Marnier-chocolate wafers, and Amaretto-laced white chocolate fondue. Friends say it's the season's hottest invitation.

Dean has hosted this party five years in a row, and he has learned some lessons along the way. The first is that every host should know just how many people he can entertain comfortably inside his home. "My house packs out with about 80 guests, and that's with all the downstairs furniture moved to a friend's garage," says Dean.

The second lesson is that if anything can be done in advance, do it. Dean's other Christmas party accomplishes just that. Five or six of Dean's closest friends come over one week before the big formal event to help him mass-produce finger foods for the following week. Like his black-tie party, Dean's preparty party has also become a holiday tradition.

How did this working get-together begin? "Well, some of my friends said, 'If you have that party, I'd be glad to help out.' So I took them up on it," explains Dean. Why do his friends come back to help year after year? Chuck Vogt, one of Dean's working-party guests, smiles as he says, "I wouldn't miss this preparty party. It assures me an invitation to next year's black-tie party."

For this host, the benefits of throwing a preparty party are twofold: it enables Dean to spend an afternoon cooking and preparing for his big party *and* to enjoy the company of his best friends.

Dean doesn't change the party fare dramatically from year to year. "I'd say 20 percent of the items I serve are new recipes. Then I change the presentation on the remainder of the food enough so that it seems like a whole new spread," he explains.

Introducing new foods, however, is a hallmark of Dean's entertaining style. "The first year I did this party, my friends weren't too sure about the caviar," Dean laughs. "But some of them tried it and found out that they liked the taste. Now, it is consumed.

"When I first started giving this party, I tried to serve too many items," he continues. "In order to simplify, I removed duplications." Instead of offering two cheeses, for example, he now serves one. "My favorite is Brie warmed inside a loaf of pumpernickel bread."

During the working party, Dean's friends assemble the most labor-intensive items on the menu. Chocolate truffles top the list of delicacies to be made. (Sampling is allowed, of course.)

Year after year, the group makes nearly three hundred pieces of spanakopita. In Dean's recipe for this classic party food, a combination of crab, spinach, and feta cheese is folded inside phyllo dough. Cookie sheets full of these two-bite hors d'oeuvres are wrapped and stacked in the freezer.

At the formal party, the spanakopita go straight from the freezer into the oven. Ten minutes later, Dean hands a tray of hot spanakopita to the first guest he sees to pass among the other partygoers. He says, "When hors d'oeuvres come out of the oven, it makes the kitchen the gathering hot spot."

Dean's party plan (on page 29) shows his timetable for throwing two successful Christmas parties. "One week before the party, I'm virtually ready," he says. "The bar is set up, except for the ice. And, with the help of my friends – my preparty party guests – the food is complete."

The night of the black-tie party, Dean greets guests as they arrive at the door.

In assembly-line fashion, Terri Keran (working alongside Dean), Millie Reed, and Chuck Vogt fold up their share of crab-and-spinach triangles. Dean tends to the chocolate truffles. For *Southern Living's* Christmas Truffles recipe, see page 113.

During his bachelor days, Jim Reed roomed with Dean. For the preparty party, he and his wife, Millie, are assigned to the chocolate detail.

Elizabeth Bailey can't remember a Christmas in Atlanta without Dean's preparty party and three hundred pieces of spanakopita.

Dean's Party Prep Schedule

Dean Brunton has a passion for entertaining. He celebrates Christmas with not one, but two outstanding parties.

Professionally, Dean is a sales engineer for Georgia Power. He serves as a consultant to large industrial clients, addressing their electrical- and chemical-related engineering concerns.

How does Dean parlay his engineering expertise into a successful party? He establishes a party prep schedule. "That's my background," he says. "Give me a schedule and I'll follow it."

Six months in advance, Dean commits to hosting the party. From that point, Dean brings together all the makings of his annual black-tie party – the guest list, the menu, and the decorations.

July
- Consults the calendar for a date to hold both the formal party and the preparty Christmas party.

September
- Makes the guest list and designs the invitations. Dean would rather spend most of his party budget on food; therefore, he allows four to six weeks for the printer to deliver his invitations rather than paying for while-you-wait service at the quick-copy shop.

October
- Begins work on the menu. Visits Mom in Columbia, South Carolina, to borrow china and silver serving pieces.

Early November
- Addresses invitations to be mailed no later than three weeks before the party date.

Mid-November
- Finalizes the menu. Assigns serving dishes to each item on the menu. Tags the dishes with a yellow sticky note so that he will remember which food goes in which dish.

Two Weeks Ahead
- Trims the tree, garlands the stair and porch, and purchases poinsettias.

One Week and One Day Ahead
- Goes grocery shopping.

One Week Ahead
- Throws a preparty party to prepare the food on the black-tie party menu. Sets up the bar.

One Day Ahead
- Moves downstairs furniture out of the house. Has tuxedo pressed.

The Tasty Tradition of Family Recipes

Try Ann Brittain's Pineapple Cake – it's a family favorite.

My mother would bring this pineapple cake to family parties, and the children would hide it so that we could have it all to ourselves," says Ann Brittain with a laugh. Tables laden with family favorites are as much a part of the holidays in Natchitoches, Louisiana, as anywhere in the South. Recipes that pass from one generation to the next are part of that heritage, and Ann has made them the centerpiece of her Christmas gift giving.

Every year, she prepares an array of old family favorites, including nut cakes, pralines, sugared walnuts, pecan divinity rolls, merliton pickles, mayhaw jelly, and loquat jelly. She puts samples of each into baskets, along with a little gift, for her friends.

The gift baskets are a family tradition that began with Ann's favorite aunt, Helen Elizabeth Williams Cloutier. "She used to bring all of us baskets at Christmas, in addition to presents," says Ann. "That's how I got started with it."

Old family recipes and Louisiana specialties make Ann Brittain's Christmas baskets distinctive and welcome gifts.

Ann inherited Beau Fort Plantation, built in 1790, from her aunt. It now serves as an annex for the Brittains' family of seven children and 11 grandchildren. One of Ann's brothers is a priest, and on Christmas Eve, he celebrates Mass with the family at a little church across the road. Then everyone comes back to Beau Fort for punch and dessert. Pineapple cake is still the favorite.

Pineapple Cake

    1 cup butter or margarine,
        softened
  ½ cup shortening
2¾ cups sugar
    6 large eggs
    3 cups all-purpose flour
  ½ teaspoon baking powder
  ¼ cup milk
    1 teaspoon vanilla extract
    1 (8-ounce) can crushed
        pineapple, undrained
      Glaze

Beat butter and shortening at medium speed with an electric mixer about 2 minutes or until creamy. Gradually add sugar, beating at medium speed 5 to / minutes. Add eggs, 1 at a time, beating just until yellow disappears.

Combine flour and baking powder; add to butter mixture alternately with milk, beginning and ending with flour mixture. Mix at low speed after each addition just until blended. Stir in vanilla and pineapple.

Pour batter into a well-greased and floured 10-inch tube pan. Bake at 325° for 1 hour and 20 minutes or until a wooden pick inserted in center comes out clean. Cool in pan on a wire rack 10 to 15 minutes; remove from pan, and let cool on wire rack. Drizzle with Glaze. **Yield 1 (10-inch) cake.**

Glaze:

  ¾ cup sifted powdered sugar
    2 tablespoons butter or
        margarine, softened
    2 to 3 teaspoons milk

Combine all ingredients. **Yield: ½ cup.**

Beau Fort Plantation, built in 1790, serves as an annex for Ann Brittain's family. The house is open for tours all year.

Volunteers with Yuletide Cheer

Savannah honors the founder of the Girl Scout movement by re-creating her family's Christmas customs.

In Savannah, Georgia, the approach of Christmas means that volunteers at the Juliette Gordon Low Girl Scout National Center are polishing their dancing shoes and tuning the piano. The house, which is the birthplace of the founder of the Girl Scout movement in the United States, comes to life with the spirit of a Victorian Christmas celebration, thanks to the efforts of these volunteer actors.

Re-creating Christmas past is their holiday tradition. Like many Southerners, they have discovered the pleasures of voluntarism at Christmastime through personal involvement – conducting tours, leading craft workshops, or performing as historical figures.

Juliette Gordon Low founded the Girl Scout movement in 1912 with a goal of promoting good citizenship and service to others. It comes as no surprise that Savannah's residents continue to support the founder's efforts through their own volunteer service at her birthplace.

Savannah Volunteers

Each volunteer shares in the commitment to furthering the education of

Juliette Gordon Low (standing center) organized the first Girl Scout troop in the United States in her hometown of Savannah, Georgia.

girls. The exact nature of each person's service at the house reflects his or her special interests.

Brownie Day, for example, requires the help of 50 volunteers. In this Saturday event, Brownie troops from the Savannah council learn how the Girl Scout founder celebrated Christmas. Children visiting on school field trips experience the same program.

Tour leaders relate that, as in many upper-middle class families of the time, the Gordons' children, including Juliette, attended school in Virginia. Because of the distance, danger, and difficulty of travel, the children rarely came home for Christmas. Letters and packages carried holiday wishes and gifts across the miles.

"Christmas gifts were modest expressions of heartfelt sentiment in the 19th century," explains Katherine Keena, program director. "The gift-giving customs included a lot of very small, handmade gifts and fewer purchased gifts."

To illustrate this point, volunteers lead children in a crafting session in which they make a small paper fan. Letters from Juliette to her mother document Christmas gifts exchanged among family members. When she was 12 or 13, Juliette made a similar paper fan for her Granny. "It is a typical gift of the period made with tinsel paper and glitter," Katherine says. "The children can take it home to decorate their trees."

The Juliette Gordon Low Girl Scout National Center

Brownie Day includes a chance to make a paper fan just like the one Juliette made for her grandmother as a Christmas gift.

With a gentle stroke of her fan across the cheek, a Victorian lady would tell her suitor, "I love you."

Photographs top and far left courtesy of the Juliette Gordon Low Girl Scout National Center

Bonnie Dawson, a staff member, and Doug Foran, a seasoned volunteer, portray guests at
the Gordons' Victorian Christmas ball, a Yuletide special event.

An Entertaining Evening

The evening rendition of Yuletide with the Gordons, an event for the community at large, casts volunteers as guests at a Christmas ball like one Juliette's parents, Mr. and Mrs. William Gordon II, might have hosted around 1886.

"People tell us this event is one of our most inviting," Katherine says. "If you pass by the house, through the windows you catch a glimpse of women in silk skirts swirling around the dance floor accompanied by gentlemen in formal attire." It is an evening for the most outgoing and theatrically inclined volunteers.

"I think these Yuletide volunteers have a secret desire to be on stage or sing or dance in public," says Bonnie Dawson, one of the program coordinators. "For some it may be just dressing in period costumes. Volunteering here allows them to do this – just a little bit, but not too much."

For Doug and Betty Anne Foran, the musical program is similar to their personal traditions. "Our principal involvement at the house is with the singing. Both of our parents were very involved in music, my mother in particular," says Doug. "Betty Anne and I are accustomed to the way in which Yuletide uses music, so performing there feels very much like an extension of our own tradition."

Doug leads carols and secular holiday tunes, inviting visitors to join in on some of the most familiar pieces. "The program really reflects what families and friends do," says Doug. "The music stops and people can talk. It's really comfortable entertaining that could be done today. For us it is wholesome, satisfying, and spontaneous. And you get to dress up!"

Dressing up for the occasion seems to delight all of the Yuletide volunteers. At least one new costume is added to the collection each year. Bonnie's own yellow silk ball gown was made from curtains that once hung in another of Savannah's historic homes, the Green-Meldrim House, which is the Parish House of St. John's Episcopal Church. "Wearing this dress makes me feel a bit like Scarlett O'Hara," laughs Bonnie.

Sherry Feathers, a Savannah restaurateur and Girl Scout leader, supports Yuletide with her skills in food preparation and presentation. She and the girls in her Cadet and Senior troops serve cider and cookies at the event.

Sherry says, "By working at Yuletide, the girls are challenged to learn about the history of scouting and about living in the late 1800s." Even these young teenagers experience a change when they don costumes. "They become very dainty and ladylike," says Sherry. "They behave as if Juliette were standing right beside them."

J. F. Pink as Mr. Gordon reads *A Visit from St. Nicholas*. J. F. and his wife, Martha, volunteer at the house year after year.

Finding Your Niche

Opportunities to volunteer are available in your own community. To find just the right place to share your talents, we suggest the following:

● Check out the special events listing in your local newspaper, or contact the chamber of commerce or visitor's bureau for a schedule of holiday events.

● Attend events that sound like fun to you or support a cause in which you have an interest. For example, if you are interested in architecture, attend programs sponsored by your local preservation society.

● Look at what the people in the program are doing, and decide what you would like to do next year.

● Call or write and offer your services.

You may not sing, dance, cook, or teach, but your organizational skills or sewing ability might be just as valuable. (Remember, the Juliette Gordon Low house tries to add one new costume a year to its collection.)

Like Doug and Betty Anne Foran, J. F. and Martha Pink, and Sherry Feathers in Savannah, you'll be creating your own Christmas tradition.

Dixie's Decorations Light Up the South

Meet the family that makes holiday trims for Main Street.

This holiday season drive down Broad Street in Selma, Alabama, walk around the square in Holly Springs, Mississippi, or catch a cab for a tour of the lights in Brunswick and the Golden Isles of Georgia, and you'll see the work of Dixie Decorations. This family-run business creates the Christmas trims that decorate the South.

Dixie Decorations was founded by Don and Augusta Lovelady in 1975 after Don took on the task of rebuilding the Christmas decorations in their hometown of Montevallo, Alabama. Today the firm buys garland and electrical wiring by the mile and tens of thousands of light bulbs for the production of the lighted displays to decorate towns and cities.

Pole decorations are the most popular type of decoration the firm produces. And Christmas trees are the most popular designs. "Our decorations are basically the same now as they've always been," says Don. "But it's like clothes, their popularity runs in cycles."

Don adds that by varying the lights and the garlands used, Dixie can give a different look to their basic designs. "The buyer sees something he likes," Don says, "but we'll make a change here and there to make it a little different."

The traditional nature of these civic decorations means designs are slow to change. When the business first began, Don would take an idea to a

Selma, Alabama, asked Dixie Decorations to build these specially designed wreaths and bows for Broad Street. Photograph courtesy of the City of Selma.

Visit Dixie Decorations and you're likely to meet most of Don and Augusta Lovelady's family – Don is third from the left, and Augusta is standing to the far right. The big red sleigh makes a yearly appearance in the local Christmas parade.

A Dixie worker puts finishing touches on an angel pole decoration. Dixie first produced this design for the resort on Marco Island, which is located off Florida's west coast, south of Naples.

welder, who would sketch the design in the dirt and build the metal frame.

Now, however, in order to build decorations that are easier for their clients to mount and store, the process is more complicated than that. Don and Augusta's daughter, Susan Fulmer, explains, "During our off-season, the girls in production come up with a lot of our ideas. Then we play with the geometry. We've got to consider the welding and lighting. We've also got to look at shipping the finished product to the buyer."

The appeal of lighted Christmas displays is growing, and ground-mounted decorations, which are similar to those Dixie Decorations makes for community displays, are showing up on the lawns of private homes, also. If you'd like more information

about acquiring some of these for your front yard, write to Dixie Decorations, P.O. Box 81, Montevallo, AL 35115; or call 205-665-1225.

Augusta's favorite decoration, an oversize Santa, currently stands outside their building. "In our early years, Don always saw to it that all the poles between downtown Montevallo and our business were filled with decorations," she says. "That Santa was on the road, and as I would drive past, it seemed to wave to me. It has a lot of personality."

This is a family business in the truest sense. The Lovelady daughters, Nan and Susan, along with Susan's husband, Jerry Fulmer, live in Montevallo and help run the day-to-day business operations. Don and Augusta's son and his family live in

another part of the state, but his children spend part of the summer in Montevallo.

Susan and Jerry's children, Fran and Chris, have spent several Christmas vacations touring the country to see final installations of Dixie's own designs and to check out the competition.

"One year, Susan and her family loaded up the van and visited 11 states," says Augusta. "The grandchildren learned to recognize the work of different companies just by how a frame was mounted on the pole."

Fran is now employed outside Dixie Decorations, and Chris is a busy teenager. Susan is proud of their pursuits and interests and pleased for the benefits of being involved in a family business. "We've had an opportunity to train our children in our business," she says, "which is something that not many people in our generation have enjoyed."

A Christmas Tradition of Historic Proportions

Making ornaments is not just a craft at Ridgeland Elementary, it's a celebration of local history.

What can you get when you combine paper, glue, paint, and a dash of Christmas spirit with the students of Ridgeland Elementary School? A history lesson in red and green!

Teachers in Ridgeland, Mississippi, have creatively turned holiday-inspired art projects into a study of community heritage. Each year, more than a thousand students, enrolled in kindergarten through fifth grade, create ornaments for the City of Ridgeland's two Christmas trees – the first at City Hall and the second in the Ridgeland Public Library.

As chairman of this annual holiday event, Ellen Dudley cheers the teachers and children for their creativity. "We select a theme for the tree. Then each teacher chooses an ornament that the class will make to decorate the tree," Ellen explains.

Teaching Never Stops

Making ornaments for the tree becomes a teaching tool used to evaluate and encourage students in a variety of grade level-appropriate skills. For the kids, however, the projects just seem like fun.

Mrs. Jamie Henderson says the Indian Bead Bells challenge her kindergarten students in two important learning areas. Mixing the salt dough by hand develops motor skills, as does forming and stringing the beads. Because the salt-dough beads are alternated on the string with green pony beads, the children also practice patterning, an important reading readiness skill. "Patterning teaches the children about letter sequences, preparing the students to read words," says Mrs. Henderson.

Discovering Hometown History

In other classes, the materials or techniques used to craft the Christmas ornaments become lessons in themselves. For example, pinecones, sweet gum balls, and magnolia leaves represent the trees that flank the Natchez Trace Parkway, the highway that follows a series of old Indian trails linking Natchez, Mississippi, and Nashville, Tennessee. To point the way along these trails, the Indians curved the trunks of young trees, training them to grow into directional markers. Following the path marked by these bent trunks, travelers could find their way through the wilderness. In the course of making a painted strawberry from a pinecone or a wreath from sweet gum balls, the children learn about these "arrow" trees, several of which still stand in Ridgeland today.

Ridgeland Elementary school work traditionally includes crafting ornaments to decorate the city's two enormous Christmas trees.

The kids at Ridgeland Elementary School wish you a Merry Christmas – squint your eyes and you will see the tree shape their red and green T-shirts make.

The Ridgeland Express steams through a student-constructed model of the 1899 Village of Ridgeland.

Re-creating the 1899 Village

Students make the model villages that are displayed at the base of each city Christmas tree from milk cartons and scraps of cardboard and paper, materials that would ordinarily be discarded. Ellen discusses with the children the different kinds of architecture and building materials that were used around the time citizens voted to incorporate Ridgeland as a village.

If you look closely at the models, you can see pride in workmanship. The paper siding and trim boards overlap to protect the building from any imaginary rain or sleet that might fall. And colored pasta decorates each exterior like evergreen garlands and Christmas candles.

"Many of the children signed their names using alphabet pasta because they were proud of what they had accomplished," says Ellen. "It is good for the students to see that when they combine all their efforts they can create something this beautiful."

Artful Lessons from Mississippi

Indian Bead Bell

The first families of the Ridgeland area were members of the Choctaw Indian Nation. Inspired by their trading beads, we made our own with simple salt-dough beads.

> – Mrs. Jamie Henderson's
> Kindergarten Class

To copy the Christmassy string of beads, make salt-dough beads according to the following recipe. Then paint the beads red and string them along a length of narrow red ribbon, alternating with green pony beads and ending with a silver jingle bell.

Mrs. Henderson's Craft Dough

> 1 cup salt
> 1 cup flour
> 1 tablespoon alum
> ¾ cup water, divided

Combine dry ingredients. Add about half the water to the dry ingredients. Knead the dough to a stiff consistency, adding more water as necessary. Pinch off the dough and roll in your hands to make marble-sized balls. To make holes in the beads, thread the balls on a wooden skewer. Bake beads in a 200° oven for 2 to 3 hours or until hard.

Note: Alum can be found in the spice section of your grocery store.

Papier-mâché Peach

Peaches played a big part in the early economy of Ridgeland. Our tiny, glittering peaches were formed from newspaper pulp and colored with layers of art tissue.

> – Mrs. Eleanor Dickerson's
> Kindergarten Class

To craft your own basket of these orchard beauties, soak 1-inch squares of newspaper in a bucket containing 1 part water and 1 part glue. The pulp is ready if the mixture feels claylike when squeezed. Mold the pulp into a peach shape. To make the hanger, insert half a paper clip into the stem end of the peach. Let dry. Cover the peach with glue and layer tiny pieces of orange, yellow, and red art tissue paper until desired "ripeness" is reached. Let dry. Coat with Mod Podge® and sprinkle with silver glitter. Let dry. To finish, glue a fabric leaf to the hanger.

Ridgeland Watermelon Slice

The economy grew as more crops, such as pecans, watermelons, and strawberries, were introduced to the area. On December 29, 1899, 150 people voted to incorporate the Village of Ridgeland. The town boasted a depot, a post office, a three-story hotel, a wagon works, a cannery, and a general store.

> – Mrs. Sharron Byrd's
> Second Grade Class

These watermelon slices have charmed the entire editorial staff of *Christmas with Southern Living*. To make your own, paint the arched side of a whole Brazil nut green. Then paint the angled sides red. Let dry. Using a cotton swab as a paintbrush, dab black "seeds" onto the red. To make the hanger, fold a 6-inch piece of ribbon in half and glue to the side of the nut – excuse us – the watermelon slice.

Decorating ★ for the Holidays

Have a Very Berry Christmas

Use lots of them – fresh and faux – for naturally wonderful decorations.

Here's a foolproof recipe for an instant Christmas look: Combine bright-red berries with lots of evergreens; add dried flowers, seedpods and grasses, gold-sprayed leaves, and grapevine, as desired. Mix well and apply to all the usual spots, such as the mantel or a sconce, and to some unexpected ones as well – the chandelier, for example, or a special piece of furniture.

That's the formula used here, at the home of J. T. Campbell and Tom Duke, owners of The Market, a group of specialty shops headquartered in Dallas.

The Market offers gifts, accessories, furniture, and dried and silk flowers, as well as interior decorating services.

Tom Duke and J. T. Campbell

At Christmas, the stores provide holiday decorating help as well. "Clients usually want something new every year," says Ben Krueger, one of The Market's floral designers. He advises them to "zero in on one look and simplify, because people usually have so much Christmas stuff that they've collected. Not using all of it every year leaves you something to work with the next year."

Campbell's and Duke's home is a good example of Krueger's approach. Mixed greenery and berries supply the theme; for variations in color and texture, he uses Chinese tallow tree berries, Spanish moss, pheasant feathers, lichen-covered live oak branches, dried hydrangea, grapevine, and gold-sprayed magnolia leaves. The results are traditional but fresh – the same sophisticated combination that characterizes The Market.

On the pages that follow, Ben shares some of his tips for re-creating the look.

Make decorating easier by starting with a ready-made garland of pine and fir. Tuck in more greenery and lots of berries for a look of abundance. Break up the horizontal line of the mantel with some verticals. An English brass-mounted horn serves the purpose here.

Take the decorations all the way to the ceiling for a spectacular effect. This massive chandelier, made from the shed antlers of English fallow deer, is crowned with 30-inch-long branches of imported holly tucked into the crevices where the antlers meet. (You can get this holly from a florist.) Pine is tucked into the chain to hide it, and grapevine and greenery weave through the bottom of the fixture.

In a small space, the chandelier may be your only decoration – it will be out of the way of guests and, because everyone can see it, it will make the whole room feel festive. A ready-made garland of noble fir, pine, and juniper wraps the post of the chandelier and swags the arms. Holly and Florida berries are tucked into the greenery, and two six-foot-long drapery cords follow the lines of the garland.

Grapevine-wrapped sconce

Decorating a sconce turns an accessory into a focal point. This wrought iron candelabra was wrapped with grapevine to provide the mechanics, or foundation, for the pine, cedar, fir, berries, and dried hydrangea.

Seven Tips for Terrific Decorations

• When decorating the mantel, combine greenery with contrasting textures and colors, such as juniper and native holly, for a richer effect than you get by using a single type of greenery. For safety, remember not to let the garland hang low enough that sparks from the fire could ignite it. As an added precaution, Krueger recommends spraying fresh greens with fire-retardant if they are to be used anywhere near flames.

• Using dried and permanent materials lets you make your fresh materials go further. Krueger used lots of artificial pepper berries to give a strong impression of color. The greenery hides the paper-wrapped stems, and the berries themselves look realistic.

• If you don't have access to deciduous Southern species of holly, such as possum-haw and winterberry, buy imported *Ilex* from the florist. It comes with the leaves removed; the berries are larger than American native holly berries and seem to cling to the branches longer.

• Raising votive candles on stands on the mantel serves two purposes: It keeps the heat from drying out the foliage too quickly and it provides a variation in levels of objects that helps make the whole display more interesting.

• If you have a handsome chandelier, draw attention to it by wreathing it with greenery and grapevines. You'll get lots of impact from this kind of decoration, and it will make the whole room feel more festive.

• When you decorate the chandelier, don't forget to ring the base of each light with a candle wreath. Purchased ones of artificial greenery and fruits will add color; add bits of fresh holly and berries or tiny pinecones.

• To make a crescent shield like the one over the bamboo hall tree, start with a chicken wire form covered with Spanish moss. Wire lichen-covered branches to this base to define the main lines of the arrangement. Fill out the shape with noble fir, juniper, native holly, rose hips, pheasant feathers, and clusters of artificial berries inserted into the base and wired in place. Thread a piece of heavy-duty florist's wire through the top back and twist to make a loop for hanging the crescent on a picture hook.

Use a crescent of greenery, berries, and pheasant feathers to call attention to a special piece of furniture, like this antique bamboo hall tree, or to accent a mirror or an interior arch.

A Grand Opening

This lavishly decorated entrance boasts a bevy of ideas.
Choose one – or all – for your own front door.

Dressed for the Kappa Kappa Gamma Christmas Pilgrimage in Houston, Texas, this house wears more than the usual wreath or garland. Three pairs of arrangements of greenery and berries lead you up the steps and to the front door. A fat magnolia garland frames the entrance, and a generous wreath calls attention to the Palladian window above. An asymmetrical swag of smilax subtly softens the overall formality. Each of the decorations is simple in itself, but layering them creates a lavish effect. What's more, the basic materials are plants you can grow yourself. For details, see below. To learn how to make each decoration, see the next page.

Growing Your Own Decorations

Tara Quigley, a Houston florist, used just a few kinds of landscape plants to create the decorations shown here. You may want to consider adding them to your yard for future Christmases.

Pyracantha: This shrub grows rapidly to a mature height of about 10 feet and should be planted in full sun or light shade. It tolerates dry weather once the plant is established. You can buy one-gallon-size container-grown plants large enough to produce fruit the first year – set them out in spring before they bloom, and you'll have berries by fall. The crop will be even bigger the second year. Remember that the berries form on wood from the previous season, so if you need to prune the plant to shape it, do so when the shrub flowers. That way, you can be sure you're not removing your supply of decorating materials.

Smilax: Several species of this climbing vine are native to the South and have become popular landscape plants for training over doorways and arbors. Most have prickly or thorny stems, but Jackson vine (**Smilax smallii**) is essentially thornless and evergreen. It grows easily in sun or partial shade and ordinary soil. To order plants, send $2 for a catalog to Woodlanders Nursery, 1128 Colleton Avenue, Aiken, South Carolina 29801.

Chinese tallow tree (popcorn tree): Native to China and Japan, the Chinese tallow tree has become naturalized along the coastal South from South Carolina and Florida to Texas. It grows in most types of soil and can withstand heat and dry weather. It is sensitive to cold, however, and although it has been grown as far north as Williamsburg, it's not reliably hardy north of Montgomery, Alabama. Plant the popcornlike seeds in pots of soil in the winter and set out the seedlings in a sunny spot in the summer, or order plants from Woodlanders Nursery (see above). Chinese tallow trees grow rapidly to a height of 35 to 45 feet. A one-gallon-size sapling from Woodlanders should be producing fruits for Christmas decorations in about four years.

Southern Magnolia: This is the essential tree for Christmas decorating, but planting one is an investment in the future, not a solution to this year's requirements. The tree is slow-growing and requires plenty of room – it can grow up to 100 feet tall and has deep roots. Plant it in a sunny or lightly shaded spot in the spring in rich soil. Use mulch to keep the soil moist, and be sure to water well during dry weather.

Low urns: Fill with florist's foam and cover with chicken wire; or, if you have planters already filled with soil, use florist's tape to secure chicken wire over the top. Push the branches through the wire into the soil. Position the magnolia low to form a bed of greenery. Next, insert the pyracantha branches so that the tallest ones shoot up and out. Balance them visually with shorter branches that go in below the magnolia and reach toward the ground.

Magnolia garland: Assemble the garland on a heavy clothesline or rope. Cut it to the desired length plus 20 inches so that the ends can drape generously on the ground. Using heavy-gauge florist's wire, attach whorls or clusters of magnolia, four at a time, working all the way around so that the garland will be very full. It is important to wrap the wire tightly, securing each stem with three or four twists. Otherwise, the garland could fall apart.

Tall urns: If you have topiaries or small shrubs planted in urns, embellish them with bunches of Chinese tallow tree berries placed around the edge of the urn. Insert apples on florist's picks above them, pushing the sticks into the soil. If you wish, spray the apples with a clear acrylic sealer. "It doesn't make the fruit invincible against the weather, but it helps," says Tara Quigley, a Houston floral designer.

Smilax garland: This is lightweight and easy to assemble – just gather up pieces of smilax of the desired length and wire them to a nail at one corner of the doorway. Tara Quigley says, "Smilax is wonderful stuff, but it has a mind of its own." Look at each piece for its form and line and let that dictate how you use it.

Wreath: Start with an artificial fir wreath 48 inches in diameter. Insert magnolia branches, smilax, and elaeagnus through the wreath to the back and wire each stem to the metal ring of the wreath form. Attach pyracantha branches the same way. Spray a pineapple with gold paint and fasten it to the wreath, wrapping wire around both the neck and the base and twisting the wires tightly at the back of the wreath.

Carriage lamps: Wire an Oasis cage (available from a florist) between the lamp and the wall and insert magnolia branches and pyracantha. The pyracantha is heavy, so you'll need to wire it to the cage. Its berries dry out quickly, but if you water the Oasis daily, they will stay plump and fresh longer.

The Lamppost

"This is a two-person job," says Tara. Get one person to hold the magnolia branches in place beneath the lamp while you secure them with heavy-gauge spool wire, wrapping tightly to keep the branches from slipping. The whorls of leaves will form a collar below the light fixture and help hold the pyracantha, which you'll need to wire to both the magnolia stems and the lamppost. (Pyracantha is thorny, so wear heavy gloves when working with it.)

To cover the post, wire smilax and more pyracantha in place to form a downward spiral around the post. Fasten each branch at the top and bottom as well as in the center, where necessary, to shape it to the post.

A Little Forest in the Foyer

It's a simply elegant way to welcome Santa to your neck of the woods.

Bring a touch of woodland magic to your entry hall with a trio of Christmas trees. This decoration would also work well in a church hall or club ballroom. These are cut trees in stands, but you could use live trees instead and plant them outdoors after Christmas.

Be sure to choose trees of different heights, and for the soft, bushy effect achieved here, use white pines. The only decorations required are tiny white lights.

To hide the stands and make a plump "collar" for the trees, stuff garbage bags with crumpled newspaper, place them around the base of the trees, and cover with fabric. Houston floral designer Becky Dossey used a paisley lamé; its rich pattern and color make a subtle foil for the natural simplicity of the trees. Working from the back of the first tree to the front and continuing around to the back of the third tree, she used a single length of fabric and tucked it around the garbage bags. To calculate the amount of fabric you'll need, stretch a tape measure around the garbage bags, starting at the back of one side and continuing to the back of the other; add three yards to allow for fullness. This is also an excellent way to cover the root balls of fresh trees. After Christmas you can use the material for another project.

Play up the trees by keeping the stair rail decoration simple and understated. Use chenille wire to fasten brass horns and heavy drapery cording to the rail. Hide the wire with gold bows.

A Chorus of Candles

Give purchased candles instant personality with these bedazzling ideas.

You could buy candles like these from a specialty shop or a catalog – or you could make them yourself for a fraction of the cost, using clothing studs, jewelry findings, and sequins to embellish pillar candles.

The hardest part of this project is making sure you have the studs properly spaced before you push them in; once the prongs pierce the wax, you won't be able to adjust the position of a stud without leaving holes in the candle.

To avoid this problem in making the tree-shaped design shown here, make a paper pattern first. Draw a triangle of the desired size. Divide the sides into equal segments (ours are at $3/8$- to $1/2$-inch intervals), mark each point with a dot, and connect the points across the tree. Divide these lines into equal segments to mark the points for the jewels inside the shape. Tape the pattern onto the candle and pierce the dots with a pin. Then remove the pattern and center the studs over the pinholes.

Star-shaped studs decorate the dark-green candle, along with cherub charms. The charms are fastened to the candle with a small bit of pliable wax. (You can also use candle adapters, which are dots of wax. They are sold in candle shops.)

To decorate tall pillar candles, look for gold or silver filigree pendants, snowflakes, or other shapes among the jewelry-making supplies at a crafts store. Combine them with sequins or pearls and secure with short sequin pins. Use sequin pins to hold pearls on top of star-shaped sequins on the red candle.

Jeweled clothing studs form a tree shape on the short, white candle, and star-shaped studs embellish the blue-green pillar behind it. The cherubs are charms secured with a bit of wax. Star sequins and pearls decorate the red candle.

All Wrapped Up for Christmas

Create these cheerful chair wraps with less than two yards of fabric.

Step into Abby Buckwald's Savannah home and you'll see a whimsical imagination at work. Old furniture gets a zingy finish when Abby wields the paintbrush, and walls wear lively patterns of curlicues and arabesques. In the same playful spirit, she covers her chairs for the holidays with cotton madras wraps.

For each of Abby's ladder-back chairs, less than two yards of dressmaker's fabric makes the wrap. Measure over the top of your chair as shown in the illustration at right to see how much fabric you'll need for each of your chairs.

Choose a lightweight fabric that drapes well. The wrong side will show on the back of the chair, so you'll want to choose a fabric that, like this madras, looks the same on both sides.

Abby Buckwald and her daughter, Kate, take a mirthful approach to Christmas decorating. Abby covered her chairs, shown at left, in vibrant madras, an unexpected but effective choice for a festive look.

Drape fabric over the chair. Catch the selvage edges where the fabric folds over the chair back. Referring to the illustration below, fold the cover so that the selvages meet at the center back. Because these covers have such an easy fit, a 44-inch width of fabric may overlap at the center by a couple of inches or it may leave a slight gap where the selvages do not quite meet. Either fit will work just fine.

Using large safety pins, fasten the right and left selvages together at the top edge and again just above the seat. Conceal the fasteners with paper-ribbon bows, like Abby uses. Or try wire-edged silk ribbon bows, or a piece of costume jewelry. Then gather the fabric on either side of the chair and knot it around the spindle. The cover will drape loosely across the chair seat.

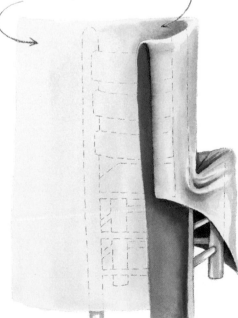

Fruit Basket Turnover

Leave out the greenery to give this traditional treatment a contemporary twist.

Fresh fruit on the mantel takes on a clean, up-to-date look when you choose a bright, sunny palette. The colors of the oranges, lemons, limes, and green and red apples used here echo the collection of majolica plates, which stay on the mantel all year. But the colors could work equally well against a range of backgrounds, from dark paneling to walls that are white, yellow, or cobalt blue. Here's how to duplicate the arrangement.

1. Lay several blocks of Styrofoam along the center of the mantel. Stack a few of them to achieve variations in height and attach them to each other with wooden florist's picks.

2. Cover the Styrofoam with sheet moss and reindeer moss (a gray-green lichen that, like sheet moss, is sold at crafts stores with the floral supplies).

3. Insert the fruits, securing them with wooden florist's picks. Be sure to balance each fruit on the front of the arrangement with one at the top or back – it's the even distribution of the weight of the fruits that keeps the whole arrangement in place on the mantel. For the best results, group 3 to 4 green apples and limes at the top and sides of the mound and fill in around them with orange and yellow fruits. This lets the eye read each color clearly. In addition, you may wish to break the line of the mantel by inserting a green apple so that it extends below the mantel.

4. To accent the focal point, add a red apple beside the one extending below the mantel edge. Balance it with another toward the back of the arrangement. Red candles reinforce this note without overwhelming the color scheme.

5. To finish the decoration, place additional lemons, tangerines, and oranges between the center arrangement and the end of the mantel. Fill in the spaces between the fruits with walnuts and tufts of reindeer moss.

A More Permanent Solution

If you want a decoration you can use year after year, use latex fruits of good quality and glue them to a moss-covered Styrofoam base.

Build a mound of fruit on the mantel by securing apples and oranges to a Styrofoam base. Carry the line of color all the way to the mantel ends by scattering individual fruits, nuts, and moss along the shelf.

Getting ready for the party is half the fun, says Bettie Bearden Pardee. To make the chair corsage, tie branches of greenery together with chenille wire and twist the wire around the chair rail. Hide the wire with ribbon.

The Art of the Party

It's all in the presentation, says entertaining specialist Bettie Bearden Pardee.

The table is as much a fashion statement as you are," says Bettie Bearden Pardee. "Don't just set it, dress it thoughtfully." The author of two books on entertaining and a popular lecturer, Bettie credits her Southern roots for her love of entertaining. Her warmth, enthusiasm, and creativity are contagious, and that's why we asked her to design a tablescape for *Christmas with Southern Living*. These pages show the results.

"Entertaining does take a lot of time and effort," admits Bettie. "A lot of it is preparation, so you might as well make the preparation enjoyable. I look at it as a pleasure." And all of the little touches – tassels on the napkins, place cards that double as party favors, distinctive handmade place mats, corsages for the chairs – help make your guests feel pampered by the attention you've lavished on them. "Small or large, formal or informal, unforgettable occasions owe their success to a devotion to details," Bettie writes.

Bettie likes to build a table's scheme on a few related elements. For this tablescape, she began with an old paisley shawl, "Cinnabar" Spode china, and cabbages. "Cabbages are my trademark, I guess," she says. "Europeans use flowers and vegetables together a lot." The cabbages, artichokes, and hydrangea topiaries supply notes of green to complement the warm, orangey reds of the shawl and china. So Christmas colors are present, but in muted, rich tones that suit the rustic setting, a 19th-century farmhouse at Starrsville Plantation in Covington, Georgia. Bettie's husband and his friend manage the plantation as a game preserve, and the Pardees sometimes celebrate holidays there.

Born in Pine Bluff, Arkansas, and raised in Beverly Hills, California, Bettie founded the *Papillon* home and entertaining mail-order catalogs in the 1970s. She has written two books, *Pardee Guide to Great Entertaining* and *Pardee Guide to Great Weekend Entertaining* (published by Peachtree Publishers), is now consulting editor for *Bon Appetit,* and lectures widely. She is also associate producer and host of an upcoming television program about entertaining at the White House.

Pardee Tips

• Dealing with limited resources, budget- or space-wise? Concentrate your creative efforts and dollars on the table. After all, this is where guests will be spending most of their time.

• Place cards are a practical assist for a hostess at a small dinner party and a necessity for guests at a larger party. Here, Bettie makes place cards that double as party favors, using jewel-toned Christmas balls.

• Fill votive glasses with one inch of water to dissipate heat from the candle. Place votive holders in the freezer for 15 to 30 minutes to make wax pop off.

• Plan effectively so that you can be cool and collected when guests appear. Few things are more unsettling to guests than the impression that their arrival has been preceded by a household commotion.

• Stick with what is familiar. Be kind to yourself and don't try a new recipe, new hairstyle or new room arrangement for a party.

• For last-minute preparations, pay attention to the details – don't worry about cleaning! Lower the lights – it creates a sense of calm and hides the dust. Put on soft music and light the candles. Straighten up any clutter, empty the wastebaskets, and fluff cushions and pillows. Clean the sink and polish the chrome in the powder room; put out a new bar of soap, a new roll of toilet paper, and fresh towels. Finally, set the table, take a deep breath, and get ready to enjoy your own party.

From *Pardee Guide to Great Entertaining,* published by Peachtree Publishers, 1990.

Details That Make a Difference

Tasseled Napkins

Embellish ordinary white dinner napkins with tassels made from 3-ply metallic thread, available from crafts stores. You will need 2 tassels for each napkin. Allow 12 yards per tassel.

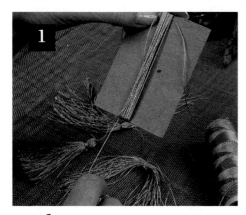

1. Cut a cardboard rectangle approximately 2 inches by 4½ inches. Holding a 6-inch length of thread at the top of the cardboard with 1 hand, begin wrapping thread from the spool around the cardboard.

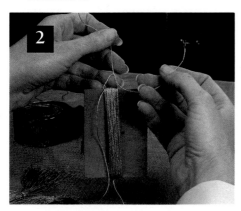

2. Wrap until the tassel is the desired thickness, ending at the bottom of the cardboard. Clip the thread. With the 6-inch thread at the top of the cardboard, tie off the tassel. Cut the threads at the bottom of the tassel.

3. Holding the tassel firmly in 1 hand, grasp the end of the thread on the spool between the thumb and forefinger of that hand and hold it tightly while you wrap the thread firmly around the neck of the tassel. Wrap 4 to 6 times. Cut and tie off. Trim the threads evenly at the bottom of the tassel.

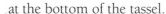

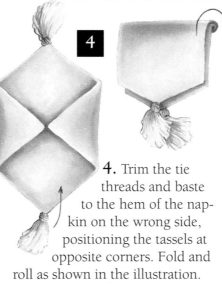

4. Trim the tie threads and baste to the hem of the napkin on the wrong side, positioning the tassels at opposite corners. Fold and roll as shown in the illustration.

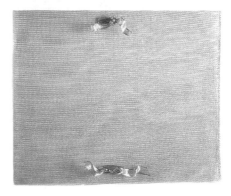

Place Mats

Purchase copper screen from a hardware store or a shop that sells plate glass and window screening. It is sold by the yard from a 54-inch-wide roll; the screen used here was purchased for about $12 per yard. Each 18-inch by 15½-inch place mat requires 2 sheets of screen, so you'll need 2 yards for 6 mats.

Using sharp scissors, cut the screen into rectangles. Center and cut a pair of holes about 2 inches apart and approximately 1¼ inches from the top of each place mat. Repeat at the bottom of each mat. Matching holes on 2 pieces of screen, tie together with gold wire-edged ribbon.

Hydrangea Topiary

Centerpiece

Vegetables and fruits in Christmas colors line the table for an easy-to-assemble centerpiece. Anchor the design at each end of the table with a hydrangea topiary.

Place a pair of topiaries in tole-painted containers and elevate them if necessary. (You can use books or box lids – the cabbages will hide the base.) Use long branches of ever-greens – Bettie used magnolia, mahonia, and cedar. Simply place them along the center of the table. If you do not use a tablecloth, rest the greenery on a runner so that it won't damage the table finish.

Place green and purple cabbages among the greenery, making sure that some face each side of the table. Gently curl back some of the leaves to create a flowerlike effect. Add artichokes, ruffly lettuce, pears, plums, and purple grapes, propping them against the cabbages and branches.

For lighting, use votive candles in clear holders. Tie gold wire-edged ribbon around each holder for a festive touch.

Fill a plastic, 3-inch-square seedling pot (or size to fit your container) with plaster of Paris. Insert a 15-inch-long dowel into the center and allow the plaster to harden. Sharpen the top of the dowel into an angle or point and push a 12-inch Styrofoam cone over the dowel. (Pierce a hole in the bottom of the cone with scissors first to make this easier.)

Starting at the bottom of the cone and dipping stems into white glue first if desired, insert stems of dried hydrangea. Clip flower heads into smaller sprigs, if necessary, to obtain a pleasing shape.

Your Centerpiece Is Served

A handsome holiday table is easy to set when you follow Grady Wheeler's recipe for success.

For a quick centerpiece, fill matching bowls and vases with color-coordinated flowers, fruits, and vegetables and assemble them on a tray.

When Grady Wheeler comes to the table with a tray, it's more likely to hold a holiday centerpiece than dinner. This Beaufort, North Carolina, floral designer came up with the idea of presenting centerpieces on trays while he was doing a program on table decorations for the docents at the North Carolina Governor's Mansion. He

Regis and Grady Wheeler work as a team when they entertain, and their personalities complement each other. "Regis is a very good ahead-of-time planner," says Grady. "I'm more of a last-minute person."

developed the idea further for programs for the North Carolina Museum of History Associates and put it to work at home for parties that he and his wife, Regis, gave.

The advantage is that it lets him assemble the arrangement in the kitchen and keep the mess of clipped stems, discarded leaves, and stray berries out of the dining room. And if a decoration needs refreshing after a few days, it's easy to pick it up and carry it back to the kitchen for a little touch-up. A tray also lets him present a variety of items as a single arrangement – a fast, effortless way to pull together a simple centerpiece.

On these pages are two examples, one casual and one formal. On the pages that follow, Grady shows how to assemble one of his favorite centerpieces on a tray.

For an informal meal or buffet, Grady and Regis like to combine

their blue-and-white Phil Morgan pottery with bright reds – peppers, gerbera daisies, crab apples, and berried branches are bold and Christmassy. The various containers are grouped on a wicker tray made by Regis's mother.

Wooden apple cones have been around a long time, Grady notes, but they continue to be popular because they are so easy to work with. The secret to a full-looking cone is to add nails to those that are already in place when you buy the cone so that there are nails one inch apart over the whole form. The nails should protrude a little more than one inch. If you don't have a wooden cone, you can use a Styrofoam cone and secure the apples and greenery with florist's picks. Grady also raised the cone shown here on a block of Oasis to provide a base for inserting greenery.

How to Assemble an Apple Cone

Begin by protecting the silver tray with a piece of plastic wrap under the block of wet Oasis. Place the cone on the Oasis and trim the corners so that they're even with the base of the cone.

Using small apples of fairly uniform size and beginning at the bottom of the cone, push apples onto the nails. Grady says, "I always start at the bottom because of the weight, and I try to alternate colors, but it won't ever work out perfectly."

Insert ivy into the Oasis, just above the tray, to follow the dimensions of the tray – longer pieces to each side and shorter pieces to the front and back. Fill in the Oasis base with six-inch-long pieces of boxwood and sprigs of variegated pittosporum and add more ivy close to the apple cone for lines that lift upward. To keep the apple cone from looking like it's floating above the greenery, insert apples on florist's picks into the Oasis. Hide the cone by tucking short sprigs of boxwood among the apples secured on nails. Finish by spraying the arrangement with plant polish.

Present a traditional apple cone on a silver tray for an elegant, formal centerpiece. The secret to a really effective cone is to add more nails to the purchased wooden form so that you can place the apples closer together.

How to Make a Hurricane Globe Centerpiece

Grady and Regis were married on Christmas Day, and their wedding china, Lenox "Pine," and an antique hurricane globe inspired the Christmas tablescape shown opposite. "I saw the lamp in an antiques shop and went ape over it," says Grady. "Regis bought it for me for Christmas."

The centerpiece is equally effective with a clear hurricane globe. Elevated arrangements are very popular now, Grady notes, and "this is a really easy way to do that." Guests on opposite sides of the table can see through the globe, and the arrangement on top is above the line of sight, so the centerpiece has a lot of impact without obstructing conversation. It also requires very few materials and is easy to assemble using cuttings from your garden or the roadside.

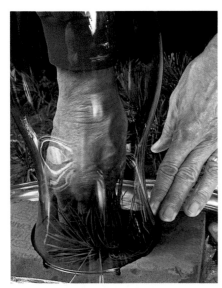

1. Cut a block of wet Oasis in half lengthwise (so that the arrangement won't be too tall) and place it on plastic wrap on a brass tray (Oasis can cause some metals to discolor.) Push the hurricane globe firmly into the Oasis and insert short pieces of pine.

2. Insert pine branches into the Oasis around the base of the globe. Keep the branches low and make sure that they follow the lines of the tray.

3. For texture, tuck small pinecones among the branches. For color, add berried branches.

4. For the arrangement on top of the hurricane globe, place a block of Oasis on a clear glass saucer and trim the top corners. This makes it easier to create a rounded arrangement.

5. Secure the Oasis to the plate by wrapping with clear floral tape or clear adhesive tape. Make sure the plate is dry so that the tape will adhere to it.

6. Insert pine branches on all 4 sides, and then into the corners and on the top. Use just enough greenery to cover the Oasis; be careful not to make the arrangement too heavy.

7. Add berries to the top arrangement and finish with ribbon wired to florist's picks. Place the plate on top of the hurricane globe and add ribbon around the base as well.

Five Fabulous Trees

We asked designers to take an ordinary grapevine tree, available from the crafts store, and create something spectacular.

The basic tree each designer used gets its shape from the heavy wire on which the vines are coiled; as a result, the base is springy and will need to be stabilized. Each one suggests his or her own way to do this.

71

A Classic Fruit Pyramid

Dorothy McDaniel and Grant May

Dorothy McDaniel has owned a florist's shop in Homewood, Alabama, for 17 years. Grant has worked with her as a designer for the last three. Dorothy's shop offers potted flowers, garden accessories, and gifts, as well as fresh flowers and custom flower arrangements. She looks for accessories that make decorating with fruits and flowers quick and effortless. "I'm into instant success," says Dorothy, "because that's all I have time for."

To make the tree:

1. To support the weight of the fruit, make a framework of chicken wire inside the spiral grapevine tree. Fill the framework with blocks of green Styrofoam, cutting as necessary to fit. The framework may extend above the tip of the grapevine tree (see photograph).

2. Hot-glue mixed nuts to green grosgrain ribbon and let dry. Using a hot-glue gun, attach the ribbon to the grapevine spiral.

3. Using wooden florist's picks, secure lemons, limes, lady apples, pomegranates, pears, and large green apples to the Styrofoam. Distribute the fruit evenly according to color and shape but concentrate the largest fruits (pears, pomegranates, and large green apples) closer to the bottom. If the fruit is ripe and soft, position the pick in the Styrofoam at the desired angle and push the fruit onto it.

4. Wire 3- to 4-inch-long sprigs of holly and spruce or cedar to florist's picks and fill in around the fruit until the Styrofoam base is completely covered.

Hazelnuts and Roses

Tara Quigley

At her florist's shop in Houston, Texas, Tara specializes in the English garden style. But she's quick to add, "We're also adept with greenery, especially native greenery, and grasses and berries. I use weird things, anything that grows in Texas."

The tree Tara designed is covered with hazelnuts, which remind her of Christmas, and with roses that she and her staff dried. Bits of broken copper Christmas balls add sparkle to each bouquet of flowers.

To make the tree:

1. Cover a 3-foot-tall Styrofoam cone with sheet moss, using low-melt hot glue to secure the moss.

2. Push the spiral grapevine tree down over the cone. Stretch it if necessary so that it hugs the cone tightly. Use greening pins (or make U-shaped pins from florist's wire) to secure the top of the tree to the top of the cone.

Base: Spiral over cone

3. Using pan-melt glue (available from crafts stores), dip hazelnuts into the glue and attach them to the cone, filling all spaces between the grapevine spirals.

4. Spray with Glossy Woodtone by Design Master or with any shiny, amber-tinted varnish.

5. Insert elaeagnus or other curving twigs to create a more interesting outline. Dip twig ends in glue and insert them into the Styrofoam, working ends in between nuts.

6. Using a low-melt hot-glue gun or pan-melt glue, apply dried roses and bits of dried hydrangea to the grapevine, clustering flowers to form bouquets. Break Christmas balls into shards and hot-glue them among the bouquets to add sparkle. Lightly spray small bunches of plastic grapes with gold paint and glue or wire them to the grapevine below the bouquets.

7. For roping, spray heavy cotton drapery cord with gold paint, tie it into a bow, and pin it to the top of the tree. Use hot glue to hold curves in place. Spray a plastic cherub gold and hot-glue it to a florist's pick; insert it into the top of the cone.

8. To protect dried flowers from softening in humid conditions, spray the entire tree with several coats of satin-finish polyurethane.

73

Tassels and Pearls

Pam Melton

Pam owns Melton Interiors, an interior decorating shop in Hoover, Alabama. A graduate of Auburn University with a degree in interior design, she worked for a Birmingham interiors firm for 10 years before going into business for herself in 1986.

Her personal signature is an eclectic look, "a tad contemporary, with a lot of color." The tree she decorated wears tassels – one of the year's top decorating accessories – and pearls, with bouquets of dyed burgundy galax leaves, dried yarrow, and dried orange slices for bold, warm color.

To make the tree:

1. Make a base for the tree by covering a 1-inch-thick piece of Styrofoam with sheet moss. Paint an 18-inch dowel gold and push it into the center of the Styrofoam. Center the grapevine tree over the dowel and wire the top of the tree to the dowel. Push branches of curly willow through the top of the tree into the Styrofoam base.

2. Starting at the top of the tree, attach pearls and gold-bead garland to the grapevine, making deep loops and wiring them in place with fine gold wire (available from crafts stores).

3. Hot-glue white drapery tassels at each point where the beads are caught up.

4. To assemble bouquets, with metallic gold ribbon, make package-topper bows. Hot-glue dried yarrow in the center of each bow and glue over the tassel cord. Attach dried orange slices and dyed galax leaves behind and around the bouquets, using a hot-glue gun.

5. At the top of the tree, glue galax leaves where curly willow emerges from the grapevine tree. On the front of the tree, glue a tassel and bouquet. At the sides, glue dried orange slices.

Base: Spiral over dowel and branches on moss-covered Styrofoam

Mossy Rings

Charlotte Hagood

Now working as a free-lance designer, Charlotte lectures on and demonstrates nature crafts and herb gardening. She joined *Decorating and Craft Ideas* magazine in Birmingham, Alabama, as a staff designer in 1979 and came to Oxmoor House as an editor about 10 years later. Her crafts projects have been featured in *American Country Christmas* and *Christmas with Southern Living* as well as other books and magazines. Because natural materials are one of Charlotte's favorite media, we asked her to work with moss. Her ribbon star is featured on page 82.

To make the tree:

1. Soak moss in water until soft and pliable. (Charlotte used a material that florists refer to as mood moss. You may substitute sheet moss for a shaggier texture and more slender spiral.) Squeeze out excess water.

2. Starting at the bottom of the tree, wrap moss around the grapevine, binding each piece of moss with florist's wire. Twist the ends of the wire together on the inside of the tree. Continue until the tree is completely covered.

3. Spray an 18-inch dowel with gold paint. Fill a wine bottle with sand to weight it, insert the dowel in the bottle, and place the bottle in the center of the tree.

4. Using $1\frac{5}{8}$-inch-wide mesh-and-gold metallic ribbon, $\frac{7}{8}$-inch-wide gold-and-white ribbon, and $\frac{3}{8}$-inch-wide purple satin ribbon, cut 4 (1-yard) lengths of each. Hot-glue the ends of the mesh-and-gold ribbon to the dowel, about 3 inches from the top, arranging them so that 1 piece is at the front of the tree, 1 at the back, and 1 on each side. Center and glue the purple satin ribbons over these. Glue the gold-and-white ribbons in between. Tuck ribbons between the coils of the tree, as shown in the photograph.

5. Make an 8-pointed star following the instructions on page 82. Glue to the top of the dowel, hiding the ribbon ends.

Base: Spiral over weighted bottle with dowel

A Victorian Confection

Jane Martin

Jane began decorating cakes in England eight years ago. The most memorable cakes that she and her partner made included one shaped like a helicopter for Sarah Ferguson, the Duchess of York, and a replica of The Mallard, the fastest steam engine in England. That cake was displayed in the York Railway Museum.

Now living near Birmingham, Alabama, with her husband and their two sons, Jane creates stunning wedding cakes covered with rolled fondant icing and decorated with exquisite gum paste flowers. She's particularly adept at creating fondant that looks like eyelet and lace. Jane receives orders for her cakes from all over the country and delivers them personally – they're too delicate to be shipped.

The tree Jane decorated for us is made entirely of gum paste, except for the grapes, which are plastic. (While fondant is edible, gum paste is not, and this tree is strictly for show.)

To order the angel cookie molds for the tree topper: call Cookie Art Exchange, 603-668-5900, and ask for information about their "Brown Bag Cookie" Art Cookie Molds. Or write to Cookie Art Exchange, P. O. Box 4267, Manchester, NH 03108.

To order ready-made gum paste: write to Wilton Enterprises, 2240 West 75th Street, Woodridge, IL 60517. You can also buy gum paste at bakeries that sell decorated cakes.

To make royal icing: Mix 6 egg whites with 1 teaspoon of cream of tartar and beat at medium speed until soft peaks form. Add 1 (16-ounce) package of powdered sugar and mix well. Add another 16-ounce package of powdered sugar and beat at high speed 5 to 7 minutes. Yield: about 4 cups.

To make the tree:

English eyelet cutters are available from shops that sell cake decorating supplies. You can also make your own cardboard template with a scalloped edge. The scallops should be about 2½ inches deep.

Do not pull the top of the tree into a vertical position. Instead, leave it horizontal and cover it with a cardboard circle to serve as the base for the angel topper. The finished tree is fragile, so you'll want to decorate it on the stand or platform on which you'll display it. Jane secured her tree to a clear acrylic platter, using royal icing, and placed the platter on a lazy Susan.

1. Stabilize the tree by inserting long cocktail sticks between the coils. Cover the grapevine with aluminum foil. Cut a piece of cardboard to fit over the top of the tree and attach it to the grapevine with royal icing. Cover the cardboard with royal icing.

2. Roll out gum paste to a thin sheet. Using an English eyelet cutter or a cardboard template, cut 6-inch lengths of eyelet.

3. Starting at the bottom of the tree and using royal icing as "glue," drape eyelet over the foil-covered grapevine, overlapping ends to cover the grapevine completely. Let dry overnight. Do not refrigerate.

4. Roll out gum paste to a thin sheet. To make a frill, use the scalloped-edge cardboard template and cut 6-inch-long strips of gum paste. Frill the scalloped edge. Using royal icing as glue, attach the frilled lace over the hardened eyelet lace, as shown in the photograph. For edging and trim, tint gum paste pale green and pipe along the edges of the eyelet and frill. Let dry for 24 hours.

5. To make ivy, dye gum paste with green food coloring. Roll out to a thin sheet. Using a small, fresh ivy leaf as a pattern, cut ivy leaves from gum paste. For stems, dip the end of a 1-inch-long piece of florist's wire into egg white and insert into each leaf. To form a vine, wrap the wire stem of each leaf with florist's stem wrap and

join stems to a long piece of florist's wire with more stem wrap. Let dry 24 hours. Bend the long wire to shape it and attach the ivy to the tree with royal icing, positioning the ivy so that it follows the spiral of the grapevine.

6. Paint bunches of small plastic grapes with egg white and dust with powdered sugar. Attach to the tree with royal icing. Let dry.

7. To make the angel tree topper, dust the cookie mold lightly with cornstarch. Press gum paste into the mold. Tap out onto a cake rack covered with waxed paper and let dry undisturbed for two days. Repeat for the second angel. Dust angels with blush or paint with food coloring diluted with a small amount of vodka or gin (the alcohol will evaporate, leaving the color in place). Using royal icing, attach the angels to the front and back of the tree top.

8. To finish, make gum paste lilies or use large fresh or silk flowers. Tuck them between the angels at the top and sides, securing with royal icing. Add ribbons as desired.

Step 1

Base: Spiral on platter, stabilized with cocktail sticks.

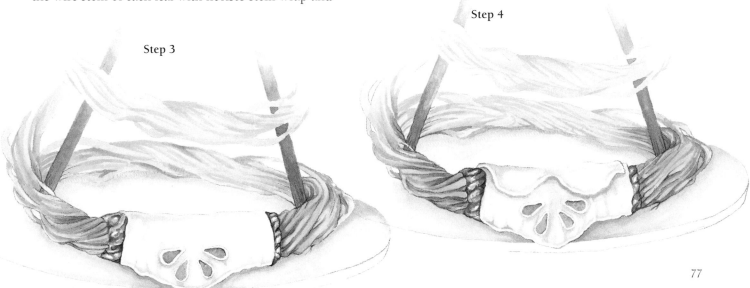

Step 3

Step 4

Christmas Treasures

Paint on the Personality

Just a few brush strokes can turn inexpensive glass dessert plates into dishes with a designer look.

Tools
tracing paper
grease pencil
#1 round paintbrush
cotton swabs

Supplies
9½"-diameter glass plate
gold leaf paint

Pattern on page 157

1. To make template, turn plate upside down on sheet of tracing paper. Trace around edge of plate. Cut out circle and fold into quarters. Transfer pattern to 1 quarter of template.

2. Using grease pencil, mark front of plate with 1 vertical and 1 horizontal line to divide plate into quarters. Tape pattern to back of plate, aligning folds in template with marked lines. Using grease pencil, transfer pattern to 1 quarter on plate front. For remaining quarters, move pattern and repeat. Remove pattern after transferring last quarter.

3. Turn plate upside down. Using gold leaf paint and paintbrush, paint design on back of plate. Using cotton swab, paint dots. Let dry. Wipe grease pencil lines off front of plate.

To clean, wash plates by hand with liquid soap and warm water. Do not scrub design on back. To store, place a paper towel between each plate.

Work in an assembly-line fashion and you'll have service for eight ready in a weekend. To show off your hand-painted dinnerware, set plates on a charger (a large flat dish or platter).

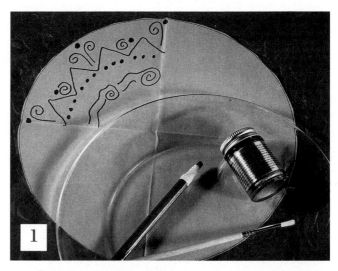

Transfer pattern to paper template.

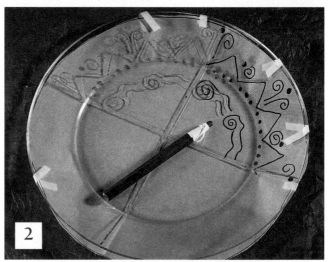

On plate front, trace design on each quarter of plate.

Turn plate upside down. Design is clearly visible through plate, so actual painting is easy to complete.

Twinkle, Twinkle, Ribbon Stars

With a few drops of hot glue and a yard or two of ribbon, you can make one of these stunning stars. Craft a whole constellation for your tree and gifts.

Tools
heavy paper
hot-glue gun and glue sticks

Supplies
ribbon:
- **for 6-pointed star,** 1 yard (1⅝"-wide) wire-edged ribbon
- **for 6-pointed stacked star,** 1 yard (1⅝"-wide) sheer striped ribbon and 26" (⅞"-wide) striped ribbon
- **for 8-pointed stacked stars,** 2 yards (1⅝"-wide) ribbon

1 (⅝") button for each star
8" piece of lamé thread (for star to hang as ornament)

Patterns and diagram on page 159

Cutting the ribbons:
Transfer patterns A, B, and C to heavy paper. Using patterns as a guide, for 6-pointed star, cut 6 As from ribbon. For 6-pointed stacked star, cut 6 As from 1⅝"-wide ribbon for large star and 6 Bs from ⅞"-wide ribbon for small star. For 8-pointed stacked star, cut 8 As for large star. From remaining ribbon, trim ½" along 1 edge to make ribbon 1⅛" wide. Cut 4 Cs from narrowed ribbon for small star points.

Shaping the star points:
Referring to diagram, shape each cut piece into a star point. Using tiny drops of hot glue, secure overlapping edges where indicated by dots.

Assembling the stars:
Setting aside small star points for 8-pointed star, arrange star points in a circle, loop side up, with glued edges pointing out. Using tiny drops of hot glue, join each point to adjacent point at center and outer edge of loops. Six-pointed star and 6-pointed stacked star will form a cup 6½" in diameter. Eight-pointed star will lie flat and measure 7" in diameter. For 6-pointed stacked star, glue small star on top of large star. For 8-pointed star, refer to photograph for placement and glue small star points on large star.

Glue button at center. For ornament, make hanger, using 8" piece of lamé thread. Fold thread in half and secure ends to back of star between 2 points, using tiny drops of hot glue.

One basic technique creates either the 6-pointed Star Ornament (bottom), the 6-pointed Stacked Star Ornament (top), or the 8-pointed Stacked Star (right).

Fragrant Pomanders Spice the Season

These pomanders, studded with cloves and anise, are new Christmas classics, a long-lasting aromatic decoration.

Tools

button hook or skewer
low-melt hot-glue gun and glue
 sticks
garden clippers
drill and 1/8" drill bit

Supplies

3"- and 5"-diameter Styrofoam
 balls
brown acrylic polymer spray paint
1/4 pound of whole cloves
1/2 pound of star anise
raffia
2 cinnamon sticks
8 fresh bay leaves
sheet moss
small pinecone
dried pomegranate
jute twine

Note: To purchase star anise, cloves, or bay leaves in bulk, check with your local health-food store or contact these mail-order suppliers:
 • Texas General Store, 2200-A Bayport, Seabrook, TX 77586, 800-982-9828.

 • Tom Thumb Workshops, Rt. 13, P.O. Box 357, Mappsville, VA 23407 804-824-3507.

For Both Pomanders

Using button hook, make hole through center of each Styrofoam ball. Paint balls brown and let dry.

Clove Pomander

Using 1/8 pound of cloves and 3"-diameter ball, press stem end of cloves into foam to completely cover ball. To make hanger, fold 3 long strands of raffia in half. Pull raffia through ball, leaving loose ends at bottom of pomander. To secure, knot loose ends around cinnamon stick; trim ends to 2".

To finish pomander, glue bay leaves at center top of ball. Glue small clump of sheet moss on top of leaves around hanger.

Star Anise Pomander

Using hot glue, apply rows of star anise around circumference of 5"-diameter ball. To cover top and bottom of ball and fill gaps between star anise, press stem end of cloves into Styrofoam, using 1/8 pound of cloves. Glue bay leaves at center top of ball.

Using garden clippers, cut away top half of pinecone and trim outside edges from top rows of bracts. Referring to photograph and using drill with 1/8" drill bit, make holes for stringing through center of trimmed pinecone, pomegranate, and cinnamon stick.

To assemble pomander, make a large knot in jute by tying 2 or 3 knots on top of each other 3" from 1 end. Fray jute below knot. Thread opposite end of jute through pomegranate, cinnamon stick, ball, and pinecone. Knot jute above pinecone to secure. To make hanger, loop twine and knot again.

Star Anise

Whole Cloves

Enjoy the Christmassy aromas of cinnamon, cloves, and star anise with a Clove Pomander (left) or Star Anise Pomander (right).

Choose Your Stitch for This Alma Lynne Angel

America's most vivacious cross-stitch designer challenges you to make the switch to duplicate stitch.

Stitchers all over the country know of Alma Lynne Hayden through her cross-stitch designs. The beautiful shading and distinctive style of her works convey a warmth and charm that are irresistible. Over the last few years, Alma Lynne has applied her designs to duplicate stitch as well and is introducing thousands of cross-stitchers to a technique once practiced largely by knitters.

"Duplicate stitch had always been the province of knitters for embellishing sweaters," explains Ed Hayden, Alma Lynne's husband and business partner. But Alma Lynne realized that it was perfect for cross-stitchers, too. "It's still a counted-thread art," she says. "You work from a chart, stitching

Cross-stitch designer Alma Lynne Hayden models a sweater embellished with her innocent, pigtailed angel. Like cross-stitch, duplicate stitch is a counted-thread technique, but the threads form a V shape instead of an X.

with floss and holding the threads at the back. Once you learn the V stitch, that's all there is to it." It's a fast and easy way to personalize a purchased sweater with a design that appears to be knitted into the garment.

For *Christmas with Southern Living,* Alma Lynne designed a rosy-cheeked, pigtailed angel that can be duplicate-stitched on a sweater or cross-stitched on a pillow. "It's easy to take a pattern for duplicate stitch and do it in cross-stitch," says Alma Lynne. "What you see on the chart is what you get when you cross-stitch it." Working in reverse, from a cross-stitch chart to duplicate stitch, however, is not recommended: the design will be distorted in unpredictable ways.

Alma Lynne is the author of two books from Oxmoor House, *Alma Lynne's Country Cross-Stitch* (1990) and *Alma Lynne's Cross-Stitch for Special Occasions* (1993), as well as dozens of paperback booklets and individual patterns. Her favorite subjects are country motifs and children, and she's constantly creating new designs. The ideas can come at any time. "Sometimes if we're in a restaurant and I get a vision, I'll write it down and draw it the next day," she says. "I don't start drawing right there. I do have a little decorum – not much, but a little! Sometimes the ideas just flow – God must be shooting them down to me, because I can't think that fast!"

Duplicate-stitched Sweater

The sample was stitched on a white, 100% cotton sweater from Alma Lynne Designs. The gauge is 6 x 8. To make the floss fluffier and bulkier for duplicate stitching, Alma Lynne recommends pulling the floss between two pieces of Velcro.

Tools
#18 or # 22 tapestry needle
crochet hook

Supplies
embroidery floss (see color key)
white long-sleeve sweater with 6 x 8
    gauge
5 yards (³⁄₄"-wide) gold-and-mesh
    ribbon
11" (¹⁄₂"-wide) white Velcro
5 yards each of the following:
    1⅝"-wide white satin ribbon
    ⅞"-wide rose satin ribbon
    ⅝"-wide navy satin ribbon

Chart and color key
on pages 154-55

Note: Plain sweaters may be ordered from Alma Lynne Designs, 611 West Broadway, Myrtle Beach, SC 29577.

Using tapestry needle and 6 strands of floss, center and stitch design on sweater front according to chart. Stitch checkerboard border 2 rows below angel and around each sleeve above cuff.

Braids: Cut 1 end of full skein of light tan floss. On right side of sweater, beginning at 1 side of lowest V stitch of hair on 1 side of face, use crochet hook to pull 1 end of cut skein from front to back. Pull end back to front at opposite side of V stitch. Pull ends of skein even and plait. Tie off tightly with floss. Repeat with another full skein for remaining braid. From gold-and-mesh ribbon,

cut 2 (5") pieces. With cut pieces, tie bow at end of each braid.

Shoulder embellishments: Cut Velcro in half. Cut remaining gold-and-mesh ribbon and other ribbons into 8 equal lengths. Separate into 2 sets, each containing 4 ribbons of each color. Center and stitch 1 set of ribbons along back side of 1 Velcro hook strip. Tie each ribbon in a loose knot to hide stitching. Trim ribbon ends at angle. Sew loop half of Velcro to shoulder seam. Repeat for remaining shoulder embellishment.

Cross-stitched Pillow

Tools
#26 tapestry needle
crochet hook

Supplies
embroidery floss (see color key)
14" x 19" piece of 25-count white
    Dublin Linen (Zweigart)
⅜ yard (¹⁄₁₆"-wide) green satin
    ribbon
40" of piping to coordinate with
    fabric
⅔ yard (44"-wide) fabric for ruffle
    and back
stuffing
⅔ yard each of the following:
    ¹⁄₂"-wide gold metallic ribbon
    ⅜"-wide rose satin ribbon
    ¹⁄₄"-wide white satin ribbon
    ⅛"-wide sage green satin ribbon
thread to match fabric

Chart and color key
on pages 154-55

Note: All seam allowances are ⅝".

Using 2 strands of floss and working over 2 threads, center and stitch design on linen according to chart.

Braids: Cut 1 end of full skein of light tan floss. Divide skein in half.

Beginning at 1 side of lowest stitch of hair on 1 side of face, use crochet hook to pull 1 end of 1 section from front to back of design. Pull end back to front on opposite side of stitch. Pull ends even and plait. Tie off tightly with floss. Repeat with second half of skein for remaining braid. Cut ¹⁄₁₆"-wide ribbon in half and tie 1 length into a bow at end of each braid.

Finishing: Trim cross-stitched pillow front to 8½" x 12⅞". With raw edges aligned, stitch piping to pillow front.

From fabric, cut 2 (6³⁄₄" x 44") strips for ruffle and 1 (8½" x 12⅞") piece for back. To make ruffle, with right sides facing and raw edges aligned, stitch ruffle strips together along 1 short edge to make 1 long strip. Fold seam allowance at each end to wrong side; with wrong sides facing and raw edges aligned, fold strip in half lengthwise. Treating both layers as 1, gather long raw edge.

With right sides facing and raw edges aligned, pin ruffle to pillow front, overlapping ends. (Piping should be sandwiched between ruffle and front.) With right sides facing and raw edges aligned, pin front to back. Stitch through all layers, leaving 3½" opening for turning. Turn and stuff; whipstitch opening closed.

For bows at pillow corners, cut each length of remaining ribbon in half. Separate ribbons into 2 sets, each containing 1 ribbon of each color. Handling all ribbons in a set as 1, make bow. Tack to 1 upper corner of pillow. Repeat for remaining corner.

As this pillow shows, when you work a duplicate-stitch design in cross-stitch, the result looks just like the chart (see page 155). It's taller and thinner than the same design worked in duplicate stitch.

Beaded Baubles for the Tree

Glue pearls and beads to geometric shapes to create these jeweled treasures.

Tools
serrated knife
short-bristle paintbrush
tacky glue
dressmaker's straight pins

Supplies (for 1 ornament)
1"-thick block of Styrofoam
selection of beads (see assortments at right)
antique gold Rub 'n' Buff®
1/3 yard (1"-wide) velvet ribbon
2 yards of narrow gold drapery cord
gold thread or embroidery floss

Using a serrated knife, cut out ornament base from Styrofoam. Diamond measures 2½" x 4¼". Rectangle is 1½" x 2¾". Diameter of circle is 2½".

Spread a thick layer of glue on 1 side of base. Drop assorted beads into wet glue until entire side is covered. Let glue dry. Apply beads to other side in same manner.

If using colored faceted beads, dry-brush Rub 'n' Buff® over beads. (If using pearls, omit this step.)

To cover edges of base, wrap ornament with velvet ribbon, tucking ends under at top and securing with pins.

Tassel: Find center of drapery cord. Working from center, wrap each end of cord around the palm of your hand 4 times. Keep lengths of cord even. Tightly bind loops at 1 end with gold thread or floss. Then pull cord ends and thread ends through pony bead. Trim excess thread above bead. Center bead with tassel over velvet

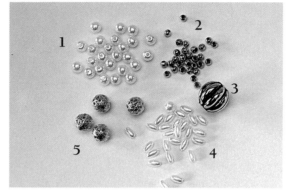

Elegance of Pearls
1. Cultured Pearls (5 mm)
2. Plated Beads (3 mm)
3. Melon Pony Bead (14 mm)
4. Cultured Pearls (3 mm x 6 mm)
5. Filigree Beads (8 mm)

Multicolored Magnificence
1. Faceted Beads (6 mm)
2. Faceted Beads (4 mm)
3. Plated Beads (3 mm)
4. Paddle Wheel Beads (12 mm)
5. Plated Beads (3 mm x 6 mm)
6. Tunisian Pony Bead (16 mm x 10 mm)

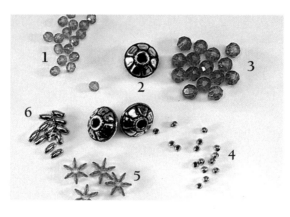

Starry Night
1. Faceted Beads (4 mm)
2. Tunisian Pony Bead (16 mm x 10 mm)
3. Faceted Beads (6 mm)
4. Plated Beads (3 mm)
5. Paddle Wheel Beads (12 mm)
6. Plated Beads (3 mm x 6 mm)

ribbon at bottom of ornament. Pull cord ends taut around sides of ornament, centering on velvet ribbon. At top of ornament, tie a knot. To keep cord from slipping, secure knot with pin. To make hanger, knot cord ends together 3" from top of ornament; trim cord ends.

Multicolored Magnificence

Starry Night

Elegance of Pearls

Beaded Baubles for the Table

Use an assortment of beads to make jeweled napkin rings as well. For each napkin ring, remove the screw eye from a 3"-diameter wooden curtain ring. Spray the ring with gold paint, and let dry. Spread glue on top of the ring; press assorted beads into glue. Let dry. If using colored faceted beads, dry-brush with antique gold Rub 'n' Buff®.

Stylish Bobs for the Tree

Press paint-coated leaves onto frosted-glass balls to make these elegant ornaments.

Tools
artist's paintbrushes:
   large, small

Supplies
fresh leaves: maple, elm, oak, or
   chrysanthemum
gold glitter fabric paint
acrylic paints: green, red,
   or purple
3¼"-diameter frosted glass
   ornaments

Select small, fresh leaves to print pattern on glass ball. Each leaf will last for 1 or 2 printings. Using large paintbrush, apply thin coat of glitter paint to underside of 1 leaf. Position leaf, paint side down, on glass ball. Gently press leaf with fingertips, making sure entire leaf comes in contact with ball. Carefully remove leaf. If part of leaf did not print, use small paintbrush to fill in these areas with glitter paint. Make 3 or 4 more evenly spaced glitter paint prints on ball.

To make colored leaf prints, mix 2 to 3 parts glitter paint with 1 part acrylic paint in desired color. Apply paint to underside of leaf and make additional prints on ball. Leave enough background space to provide a pleasing contrast to painted areas. Let dry.

More Leaf Printing

When you have finished the ornaments, you'll want to embellish other holiday necessities with leaf prints. Try these applications.

On package wrap:

To create your own signature wrapping paper for the season, experiment on plain brown craft paper, white butcher paper, and foil or tissue gift wrap. To leaf-print on paper, follow the same steps as for printing on glass ornaments. Applying the technique to large sheets of paper can be time-consuming, however, so you may want to wrap packages first and then embellish with prints. Want a custom-printed ribbon to tie up those packages? Use tiny leaves to decorate wide, satin ribbon.

Make coordinating gift-tags by printing randomly on card stock or heavy craft paper. Cut the paper to the desired size after printing – the partial shapes will add interest to the tag.

On table linens:

Leaf printing can also easily be applied to cloth or to table linens, using fabric paints. For printing on fabric, we offer these suggestions to assure your success.

● Select cloth or purchase ready-made napkins and tablecloths made from natural fibers, such as cotton or linen.

● To flatten twisted or curled leaves before printing with them, press between sheets of waxed paper, using a warm iron.

● Work on a smooth, flat surface and protect the area with plastic, cardboard, or newspaper.

● Follow manufacturer's instructions to dry fabric paint thoroughly and then heat-set the paint to make the design permanent.

● Fabric paints can withstand repeated gentle washing without peeling or fading.

A Tree Skirt and Stocking from Battenberg Lace

Who would guess our beautiful decorations are made from a tablecloth and a place mat?

Battenberg Lace Stocking

Supplies
1 (14" x 21") place mat with Battenberg lace corners
1/3 yard of white linen
white pearl cotton
white thread
1 yard (3/8"-wide) white satin ribbon
1 yard (1"-wide) white satin ribbon
1 (1 1/2") mother-of-pearl button

Pattern and diagram on page 156

Finished size: Approximately 15" long
Note: All seams are 1/4".

Referring to diagram, transfer stocking pattern to right side of place mat and cut out for stocking front. Cut off 2 lace corners for cuffs as shown in diagram. Transfer stocking pattern to linen and cut out for stocking back. From remaining linen, cut 1 (2 1/4" x 13") strip for binding and 1 (2" x 8") strip for hanger.

With wrong sides facing and raw edges aligned, pin stocking front to back. Cut 3 (37") lengths of pearl cotton. Beginning at top right, position all 3 lengths of pearl cotton on stocking front along outside edge. Machine-satin-stitch over pearl cotton around stocking edge.

To make lace cuffs, pin small pleats across cut edge of 1 lace corner, adjusting to fit stocking top. With raw edges aligned, baste cuff to right side of stocking front. Repeat to baste remaining cuff to stocking back.

To bind raw edges, with wrong sides facing, fold 2 1/4" x 13" strip in half lengthwise and finger-press; open fold. With right sides facing and raw edges aligned, stitch strip to stocking top over cuff, overlapping ends of strip. On remaining raw edge, turn 1/4" to wrong side. Fold binding over seam allowance to inside of stocking. Slipstitch folded edge to seam inside stocking.

To make hanger loop, fold each long raw edge of 2" x 8" strip 3/8" to wrong side. Then, with wrong sides facing and folded edges aligned, fold strip in half lengthwise; press. Topstitch close to edge of strip along both long sides. Fold strip in half to form a loop and stitch inside stocking back next to seam.

Referring to photograph, tie satin ribbons into bow and tack bow to top center of stocking front over cuff. Tack button to center of bow.

Battenberg Lace Tree Skirt

Supplies
1 (68"-diameter) Battenberg lace tablecloth
white thread
7/8 yard of white double-fold bias quilt binding
1 3/4 yards (3/4"-wide) white satin ribbon
6" (1/2"-wide) white Velcro

Finished size: 68" diameter

For opening, cut a 9"-diameter circle at tablecloth center. Staystitch 1/4" from raw edge around circular opening. Lay tablecloth flat; then cut a straight line from outer edge to inner circle. Along each straight cut edge of opening, turn 1/2" twice to wrong side; topstitch.

With right sides facing and raw edges aligned, stitch bias binding to staystitched inner circle. Turn raw ends of bias binding to wrong side. To create casing, fold bias binding to wrong side of tree skirt, aligning folded edge with stitching line; slipstitch. Thread satin ribbon through casing. To fasten skirt opening, cut Velcro in half and stitch strips in place along each side of opening.

Caring for Battenberg Lace

You'll probably want to launder your Battenberg linens before storing them. Elaine Harvey, textile analyst at the International Fabricare Institute in Silver Spring, Maryland, recommends washing them by hand in warm water or machine-washing on the gentle cycle. If you use bleach, be sure to use a nonchlorine variety – look for the ingredient sodium perborate on the label. Line-dry and press while damp, or dry in the dryer and remove immediately.

If pine resin gets on the tree skirt, Elaine suggests spot-cleaning it with a liquid household cleanser such as Fantastic or Formula 409. Wet the fabric, dab on the cleanser, and rub the area under running water until the spot disappears. Rinse thoroughly and launder immediately; otherwise, the cleanser may leave a permanent ring.

To store, wrap the tree skirt and stocking in white tissue paper before folding them and place them in an airtight container away from light.

Crocheted Christmas Cottage

Measuring just 3" from base to rooftop, this lilliputian house is quick to crochet.

Tools

size D crochet hook
tapestry needle
embroidery needle
serrated knife
white glue

Supplies

size 5 pearl cotton : 2 (50-yard) balls
    each red and green
1 (2" x 3" x 3½") block of Styrofoam
scraps of white felt
green and red embroidery floss or
    colored fabric markers

Base: Row 1: With 2 strands of red thread held together as 1, ch 15, sc in 2nd ch from hook and each ch across, ch 1, turn. **Rows 2–10:** Sc in each st across = 14 sc, ch 1, turn. **Row 11:** Sc in each of next 13 sts, * (sc, ch 1, sc) in last st (for corner), sc in each st across edge to next corner, rep from * around, ending with (sc, ch 1) in beginning corner, sl st in first sc of row, ch 1, turn.

Sides: Row 12: Working around post of each st, sc in each st around,

end with sl st in first sc, ch 1, turn. **Rows 13–19:** Sc in each st around, end with sl st in first sc, ch 1, turn. **Row 20:** Sc in each of next 8 sts, turn. **Row 21:** Sc in each of next 7 sts, skip last st, turn. **Rows 22–26:** Continue in same manner, working 1 fewer sc each row, turn. Fasten off after row 26.

With right side facing, join thread in corner st at opposite end of house, ch 1, rep row 20. Rep rows 22–26. Do not fasten off after last row.

Edging: With right side facing, sc around top edge of house, ending with sl st in first sc. Fasten off.

Roof: Row 1: With 2 strands of green thread held together as 1, ch 15, sc in 2nd ch from hook and each ch across, ch 1, turn.

Rows 2–23: Sc in each st across = 14 sc, ch 1, turn.

Row 24: Rep row 11 as for base. Fasten off.

Assembly: Using crocheted house as a guide and cutting with a serrated knife, shape Styrofoam to match roof peak of house. Insert Styrofoam into

crocheted house. Position crocheted roof on house top. Using green pearl cotton, slipstitch roof to house.

To make hanger, thread tapestry needle with 12" length of green pearl cotton. Pull needle through roof peak at center. Knot thread ends together.

On white felt, mark 1 (³⁄₈" x ⁷⁄₈") door and 2 (³⁄₈"-square) windows. Using 2 strands of green floss, make French knots on door for wreath. Using 2 strands of red floss, stem-stitch outlines of door and windows and bow on wreath. Or, if preferred, draw details on felt with fabric markers. Cut out door and windows, leaving a ¹⁄₈" allowance along each edge. Referring to photograph, glue doors and windows in place.

Crochet Abbreviations

ch—chain
rep—repeat
sc—single crochet
sl st—slip stitch
st(s)—stitch(es)

Knit a Wreath for the Holidays

This ring of Nordic holly is a good project for an intermediate knitter and an easy one for an expert.

Tools
size 7 (24"-long) circular needle
 (or size to obtain gauge)
2 (size 7) double-pointed needles
tapestry needle

Supplies
worsted-weight wool: 3½ ounces
 of green, 2 ounces each white
 and red
stuffing

Chart and color key on page 157

Finished Size: Approximately 14" in diameter

Gauge: 10 sts and 11 rows = 2" in St st.

Note: To change colors, wrap old yarn over new so that no holes occur. Carry color not in use loosely across the back, twisting it around working yarn every 3 or 4 sts to avoid long floats.

Wreath front: With white and circular needle, cast on 224 sts. Connect and k in the rnd. Work according to chart and color key, beginning in center of chart at A and reading from

right to left. After working last st as shown at left edge of chart, begin reading same row from right edge to middle. Continue working as established, rep pattern as necessary until all sts have been worked (pattern rep = 28 sts). At end of each rnd, you will be in middle of chart to begin next rnd. Dec sts: Column of squares at right edge of chart represents dec sts. All dec will be worked on these sts. To work dec at each edge of chart on rnds 4, 7, 10, 13, 16, 19, 22, 24, 25, 26, and 27, work a double decrease (dbl dec) in indicated color as follows: Sl next 2 sts together as if to k. K next st. Pass 2 sl sts together over st just made (1 dbl dec made). When chart is completed (after rnd 29), bind off remaining 48 sts.

Wreath back: With green and circular needle, cast on 224 sts. Work according to chart, beginning at B and dec as established for wreath front, but omitting color changes.

Berries (make 32): With red and 2 double-pointed needles, cast on 5 sts. Slide sts to right end of needle. Pull yarn tightly across back of work and k 5 sts. Cut yarn, leaving a 6" tail. Thread tapestry needle onto tail of yarn. Thread sts off double-pointed needle and onto tapestry needle from right to left. Pull yarn tightly and insert needle through first 2 sts again. Insert needle through center of berry from top to bottom. Rep to make 31 more berries.

Edging: With green and 2 double-pointed needles, cast on 5 sts. * Do not turn. Slide sts to right end of needle. Pull yarn tightly across back of work and k 5 sts (this makes a small tube of sts). Rep from * until piece measures 40" from beginning or length required to fit around outside diameter of wreath. Bind off all sts.

Note: To make sts more even, roll finished tube between your hands as if you were making a snake out of clay.

Bow: With red and 2 double-pointed needles, cast on 5 sts. Work as for edging until piece measures 27" from beginning. Bind off all sts. Gather each end of tube, pull up tightly, and secure thread.

Finishing: Referring to photograph for placement, stitch berries to wreath front. With right sides facing, stitch outside edges of wreath together. Turn and stuff. Turn under inside edges of wreath and stitch together. Stitch edging around outside edge of wreath. Match and graft edging ends together. Tie red tube in a bow and stitch to wreath front (see photograph for placement).

Knitting Abbreviations
dec—decrease(s)
k—knit
rep—repeat(ing)
rnd(s)—round(s)
sl—slip
st(s)—stitch(es)
St st—stockinette stitch

Pint-size Piñatas

Our miniature piñata-inspired ornaments hold no treats–they're made from layers of cardboard–but are sure to make your friends shout ¡Olé!

Tools
white glue stick
scissors

Supplies
corrugated cardboard
sisal twine
raffia
crepe paper streamers: green, red, white, fuchsia, yellow

Patterns on page 158

1. For each ornament, transfer desired pattern to cardboard 6 times and cut out. For hanger, cut a 6" length of twine and knot ends together. Glue 2 shapes together, sandwiching knotted end of hanger between them. For corn, also slip several lengths of raffia between shapes at end opposite hanger to make corn silks. Split raffia into thinner strands if desired. Trim remaining shapes to create 2 sets in graduated sizes. Stack and glue to each side of first pair. Let dry.

2. To hide corrugated edges of cardboard, cover tip of pepper and top and toe of boot with scraps of crepe paper.

3. Cut 12" lengths of crepe paper streamer lengthwise into thirds. Fringe 1 edge of each third. (You can stack several lengths and fringe edges at the same time.) Working from bottom to top, apply glue to cardboard and then wrap shape with fringed crepe paper strips, overlapping fringe so that no cardboard shows through.

To finish pepper, make leaves. For each leaf, cut a 3" piece of green streamer in half on the diagonal. Handling the 2 triangles as 1, pinch and twist the short side to make stem end of leaf. Apply glue and tuck leaf into ornament at hanger. To finish corn, from green streamer cut 2 pairs of leaves for husk, apply glue, and wrap 1 pair around each side of ear at hanger.

Glue two sets of graduated cardboard shapes together with twine hanger sandwiched between them.

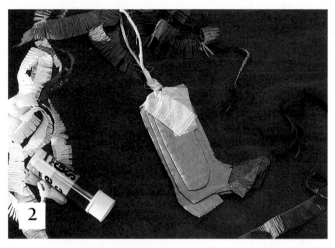

To cover corrugated edges at top and toe of boot (and bottom of pepper), glue small scraps of crepe paper over edges.

Wrap ornament from bottom to top with fringed crepe paper, overlapping so that no cardboard shows. For boot, wrap from toe to heel; then, beginning again at heel, wrap up leg to top.

Ho-ho Holiday Jewelry

A few twigs, a little paint, and you can whip up a set of folk-art Santas to wear.

Tools
saw
whittling knife
sandpaper
paintbrushes
drill and ⅛" drill bit
craft glue

Supplies
⅜"-diameter twigs or wooden
    dowels
acrylic paints: light flesh, deep red,
    black, antique white, white
felt-tip permanent markers:
    black, red
1 yard of narrow white satin
    cording for necklace
⅜"-diameter wooden beads for
    necklace: 6 green, 10 white
barrette bar or bar pin
wooden craft stick for pin

Finished size of barrette or pin:
about 2¾" wide
    Note: Let paint dry between coats.
    Saw twigs or dowels into 2" to 3"
lengths for necklace or 2" lengths for
barrette or pin. You will need 5 Santas
for necklace and 7 for barrette or pin.
With knife, scrape twigs until smooth;
round off top and bottom edges. If
using dowels, sand edges lightly.

Paint as follows:
1. Paint face light flesh.

2. Paint twig or dowel red around
face, leaving space for beard
unpainted. Paint hands black.

3. Paint hair and cuffs antique
white. Outline arms in black.

4. Paint beard white. Draw eyes
and mouth with markers.

To assemble necklace, drill a hole
from side to side through each piece,
just above Santa's hands. Referring to
photograph, string 5 Santas onto satin
cord, alternating with beads. Adjust
cord to desired length and knot ends.
    To assemble barrette, glue 7 Santas
to top of barrette bar.
    To make pin, cut wooden craft
stick to measure 2⅝" and paint red.
Glue stick to bar pin and glue 7 Santas to stick.

1   **2**   **3**   **4**

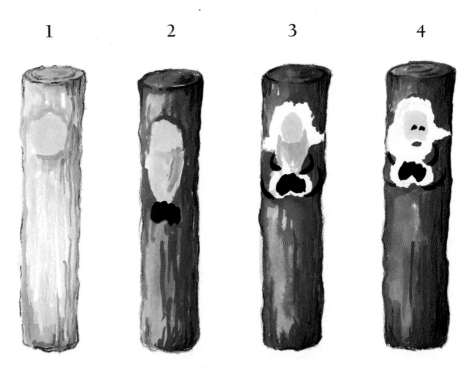

An Angel from the Garden

A casual stroll through your yard or the woods rewards you with a bounty of materials to make your own Southern garden angel.

Gathering Natural Materials

Before you begin this project, gather and dry a variety of grasses, leaves, flowers, mosses, berries, and lichens to robe the angel. The following list provides a starting point for materials to use:

For sleeves, use corn husks or wild and ornamental grasses such as straw, wheat, barley, wild oat, or pampas grass.

For petticoat, collect long-stemmed flowers such as larkspur, lavender, pennyroyal, or statice.

For skirt and wings, try leaves such as bay laurel, red maple, oak, long-needle pine, maidenhair fern, myrtle, or magnolia.

For decorating robes and head, harvest materials such as mosses, strawflowers, lunaria, pepper berries, lichens, hydrangea blossoms, yarrow, or Queen Anne's lace.

Tools
craft glue

Supplies
2 wooden chopsticks or 2 (8"-long) $\frac{1}{8}$"-diameter dowels
1 ($1\frac{1}{8}$"-diameter) wooden drawer pull
raffia
dried corn husks or dried grasses
dried pennyroyal or other long-stemmed dried flowers
dried oak, magnolia, and Southern maidenhair fern, or other dried leaves
dried lichen or other dried materials

Finished size: About 18" long

To prepare dried materials for use: Soak stems in water until they become pliable. This makes materials such as corn husks, lavender stems, and grasses easier to handle.

To make angel's head and body: Coat tip of 1 chopstick with glue and fit it into drawer pull. (If you are using dowels, you may need to sharpen 1 end of dowel to fit into drawer pull.) To create angel's arms, position second chopstick across first, $1\frac{1}{2}$" below drawer pull. Using raffia, bind sticks together.

Sleeves: Cover arms with corn husks. Using raffia, tie sleeves at each end and at center where sticks cross. To form bodice, use individual oak leaves to cover shoulders. Using raffia, secure leaves at waist.

Petticoat: Position an upside-down bouquet of pennyroyal or other dried flowers around waist, concealing lower portion of stick. Arrange oak leaves to cover stems of pennyroyal and form skirt. To secure skirt, apply glue to ends of stems and position ends close to waist. Using raffia, tightly wrap angel's waist to conceal stem ends and glue, knotting raffia securely at back.

Wings: Place a piece of fern on each magnolia leaf and position on angel's back. Apply glue to ends of stems used in wings and, using raffia, once again wrap angel's waist to conceal stem ends, knotting raffia at back. To make hanger, knot ends together 3" from first knot at waist. Trim ends of raffia.

To finish: Decorate angel's head with lichen or other dried materials.

Chopsticks and a round drawer pull form the structural frame of the angel. Shown here are alternatives for her wings and robes – magnolia leaves, fern, and larkspur instead of the oak leaves and pennyroyal shown opposite.

Celebrations
from the Kitchen

Can a Black-Tie Affair Be Easy to Prepare?

Yes, it can – and here are the recipes to prove it.

Mini Cheese Balls

    4 cups (16 ounces) shredded Cheddar cheese
    2 (8-ounce) packages cream cheese, softened
    4 ounces crumbled blue cheese
    1 tablespoon white Worcestershire sauce
1 to 2 teaspoons garlic powder
    ½ teaspoon hot sauce
    2 cups finely chopped walnuts
    ½ (15-ounce package) refrigerated piecrusts

Position knife blade in food processor bowl; add first 6 ingredients. Process until smooth. Chill for 1 hour, if necessary.

    Shape into 1-inch balls; roll in nuts. Cover and chill until serving.

    Unfold pastry, and press out fold lines. Cut with a leaf-shaped cutter; cut vines out of remaining pastry. Place on a baking sheet.

    Bake at 350° for 10 minutes or until lightly browned.

    Arrange cheese balls on serving piece to resemble a bunch of grapes; add pastry leaves and vines. **Yield: 25 to 30 servings.**

Note: If desired, make extra pastry leaves to serve as crackers with the cheese balls.

These appetizers are substantial enough to make a meal, without being too heavy or rich. Clockwise from center front: Mini Cheese Balls arranged like a cluster of grapes, Stuffed Grape Leaves, Glazed Pork Appetizers with Sweet Potato Biscuits, and Savory Canapés. For flower arrangement how-to, see page 113.

Glazed Pork Appetizers

    1 (12-ounce) jar orange marmalade, divided
    3 tablespoons Madeira
 1½ tablespoons butter or margarine, melted
    1 tablespoon stone-ground mustard*
    4 (¾-pound) pork tenderloins, trimmed
      Vegetable cooking spray
      Sweet Potato Biscuits

Combine ⅓ cup marmalade, wine, and butter; set aside.
    Stir mustard into remaining marmalade; set aside.
    Place tenderloins on a rack coated with cooking spray;
place rack in broiler pan.
    Brush with half of marmalade-wine mixture, and cover
with aluminum foil.
    Bake at 325° for 15 minutes. Uncover, and brush with
remaining marmalade-wine mixture.
    Bake 10 additional minutes or until a meat thermome-
ter inserted into thickest portions registers 160°. Cut into
½-inch-thick slices.
    Serve with Sweet Potato Biscuits and remaining
marmalade-mustard mixture. **Yield: 6 dozen appetizers.**

*1⅓ teaspoons prepared mustard may be substituted.

Sweet Potato Biscuits

    3 large sweet potatoes*
    3 packages active dry yeast
   ¾ cup warm water (105° to 115°)
 7½ cups all-purpose flour
    1 tablespoon baking powder
    1 tablespoon salt
 1½ cups sugar
 1½ cups shortening

Bake sweet potatoes at 375° for 1 hour or until done. Let
potatoes cool to touch; peel and mash. Set aside 3 cups,
and keep warm.
    Combine yeast and warm water in a 1-cup liquid mea-
suring cup; let stand 5 minutes.
    Combine flour and next 3 ingredients in a large bowl;
cut in shortening with a pastry blender or fork until mixture is crumbly. Add yeast mixture and sweet potatoes,
stirring until dry ingredients are moistened.
    Turn dough out onto a lightly floured surface; knead 5
minutes. Place dough in a lightly greased bowl, turning

to grease top; cover and refrigerate 8 hours or overnight, if
desired.
    Roll dough to ½-inch thickness on a lightly floured
surface; cut with a 2-inch round cutter. Place on ungreased
baking sheets; cover and let rise in a warm place (85°),
free from drafts, 30 minutes or until almost doubled in
bulk.
    Bake at 400° for 10 to 12 minutes or until lightly
browned. **Yield: 7 dozen.**

*3 cups canned, mashed sweet potatoes may be substituted.

Note: Unbaked biscuits may be frozen up to 1 month. To
serve, let thaw 30 minutes; cover and let rise in a warm
place, free from drafts, 30 minutes or until almost doubled
in bulk. Bake as directed.

Savory Canapés

    2 dozen unpeeled, medium-size fresh shrimp
      (about ⅔ pounds)
   16 slices thin sandwich bread
    2 (4-ounce) containers garlic-and-spice-flavored
      Alouette cheese,* divided
   ¼ cup bean sprouts
    3 pimiento-stuffed olives, sliced
    1 carrot, finely shredded
    2 radishes, sliced
    1 cucumber, sliced
    1 teaspoon capers
      Fresh parsley

Bring 6 cups water to a boil; add shrimp, and cook 3 to 5
minutes or until shrimp turn pink. Drain well; rinse with
cold water. Peel and devein shrimp; chill.
    Remove crust from bread; cut each slice into 4
triangles. Cover with a slightly damp towel to prevent
bread from drying out.
    Spread triangles with half of cheese. Set aside.
    Spoon remaining cheese into a decorating bag fitted
with a small star-shaped tip, and pipe cheese onto each
sandwich. Top with shrimp, sprouts, and remaining ingredients as desired. **Yield: 64 party sandwiches.**

*2 (4-ounce) containers herb-flavored cream cheese may
be substituted, if desired.

Stuffed Grape Leaves

2 (16-ounce) jars grape leaves
2 (6¼-ounce) packages long-grain and wild
    rice mix, uncooked
2 (14½-ounce) cans ready-to-serve chicken
    broth
½ cup Chablis or other dry white wine
2 to 3 cloves garlic, pressed
    2 tablespoons chopped fresh parsley
    1 teaspoon ground cinnamon
    1 teaspoon dried oregano
½ teaspoon ground nutmeg
¼ teaspoon ground red pepper
½ cup pine nuts
¼ cup olive oil
    2 tablespoons lemon juice
    1 cup water
    Garnish: lemon slices

Wash grape leaves thoroughly and drain; remove stems, and set aside.

Remove seasoning packet from rice; reserve for other use. Combine rice, chicken broth, and next 7 ingredients in a large saucepan.

Bring to a boil; cover, reduce heat, and simmer 20 to 25 minutes or until rice is tender and liquid is absorbed.

Stir in pine nuts, and let cool.

Place each grape leaf, vein side up, on a flat surface, reserving any torn leaves. Spoon 1½ tablespoons of rice mixture into center. Roll up tightly, folding in sides. Repeat with remaining grape leaves and rice mixture.

Line bottom of a 6-quart Dutch oven with torn or remaining leaves to prevent stuffed leaves from sticking or scorching.

Arrange stuffed leaves in even layers in Dutch oven. Pour oil, lemon juice, and water over leaves, and place a small heavy plate inside Dutch oven on top of stuffed leaves.

Cook over medium-low heat for 30 minutes. Garnish, if desired. **Yield: 5 dozen.**

Note: Lettuce leaves may be used to line Dutch oven.

How to Set Up a Coffee Bar

Treat your guests to flavored coffees – and let them choose the flavors! To set up a coffee bar, place the coffee maker on a countertop or sideboard, where you'll have room for cups, saucers, spoons, and a variety of flavoring ingredients. In addition to plenty of fresh coffee, a well-stocked bar should include:

Liqueurs
Kahlúa or crème de cacao
Truffles (a mild, chocolate-flavored liqueur)
Amaretto (almond flavored)
Brandy
Cointreau (orange flavored)
Grand Marnier (another
    orange-flavored liqueur)
Irish Mist
Frangelica (hazelnut flavored)

Other Ingredients
Cream
Granulated raw sugar
Sugar cubes
Chocolate shavings
Ground nutmeg
Cinnamon sticks
Whipped cream

For a sweet ending, offer Christmas Truffles and Strawberries with White Chocolate Cream served in a chocolate cabbage bowl. To make the tabletop Christmas tree, see page 113.

Strawberries with White Chocolate Cream

   1 **large head cabbage**
   1 **(24-ounce) package chocolate-flavored candy
       coating**
   1 **quart fresh strawberries**
      White Chocolate Cream

Remove large outer leaves of cabbage; set aside.

   Trim core end of cabbage to form a flat base. Using a sharp knife, carve out center of cabbage, leaving a shell about 1 inch thick to hold White Chocolate Cream. Set aside.

   Melt candy coating in a heavy saucepan over medium heat, stirring often. Remove from heat; place saucepan in a larger pan, and add hot water to depth of 1 inch.

   Using a pastry brush, spread candy coating on back side of 8 to 10 reserved large leaves to within ¼ inch of edges. Drape coated leaves over a bowl or glass to allow leaves to harden into rounded shapes.

   Spread candy coating over outer surface of cabbage bowl; set aside to harden.

   Peel each cabbage leaf away from chocolate leaf, starting at stem end. (Reserve broken pieces to use when assembling.)

   Arrange chocolate leaves around chocolate-covered cabbage bowl. Fill bowl with White Chocolate Cream. Arrange strawberries around chocolate leaves.
Yield: 30 appetizer servings.

White Chocolate Cream:

   1 **(4-ounce) white chocolate bar,
       chopped**
  ⅔ **cup sweetened condensed milk**
   1 **cup whipping cream**

Place white chocolate in a microwave-safe, medium-size bowl; microwave at MEDIUM (50% power) 1½ minutes or until chocolate melts, stirring after 30 seconds.

Stir in condensed milk and whipping cream; cover and chill about 1 hour or until cold.

Beat at high speed with an electric mixer until thickened. (Mixture will not be stiff.) Spoon into cabbage bowl. **Yield:** 2¾ cups.

Christmas Truffles

   1 **cup semisweet chocolate morsels**
   ⅓ **cup rum**
   ⅓ **cup grated orange rind**
   ¼ **cup orange juice**
   1 **(9-ounce) package chocolate wafers, crushed**
   2 **cups sifted powdered sugar**
   1 **cup finely chopped pecans**
   ¼ **cup cocoa**

Microwave chocolate morsels in a glass bowl at MEDIUM (50% power) 2 minutes, stirring after 1 minute.

Stir in rum and next 5 ingredients. Cover and chill at least 2 hours.

Shape mixture into 1-inch balls; roll in cocoa. Store in the refrigerator. **Yield: 7 dozen.**

Make It Easy on Yourself

Some of these recipes are time-consuming, but none are difficult. Take the stress out of preparation with this make-ahead plan.

One Month Ahead:
• Make and freeze unbaked Sweet Potato Biscuits.

One Week Ahead:
• Make Christmas Truffles.

Three Days Before the Party:
• Make Stuffed Grape Leaves.

Two Days Before the Party:
• Make Mini Cheese Balls and White Chocolate Cream.

The Day Before the Party:
• Prepare the glazed pork and the chocolate cabbage bowl.

The Day of the Party:
• Prepare Savory Canapés and pastry leaves for Mini Cheese Balls; wash the strawberries. Thaw Sweet Potato Biscuits, let rise, and bake as directed.

A Little Something for the Sideboard

To make the buffet flower arrangement on page 108: Start with a purchased ivy topiary, trained in a basket shape with a pot in the center. Fill the pot with Oasis. Cut the foliage off of a pineapple and hollow out the center of the fruit. Spray the outside copper and secure the fruit to the top of the Oasis with florist's picks. Arrange flowers as desired in the Oasis and the pineapple, using the pineapple as a vase.

To make the tabletop Christmas tree on page 112: You'll need 2 blocks of Oasis, chicken wire, Arrange-It™ foam (available from crafts stores), a terra-cotta pot, and cuttings of pine and cedar. Wrap the blocks

of Oasis with chicken wire. Following manufacturer's instructions, spray Arrange-It™ into the pot and push the Oasis into it. The foam expands as it hardens, forming a solid base for the tree. Let the foam dry and then plunge the entire form into water to soak the Oasis. Drain, then insert sprigs of evergreens to create the tree shape.

To decorate the tree, insert roses, narcissus, and variegated holly into the Oasis base. For the tree shown here, 2-inch bubble vases were wired to florist's picks and inserted into the base; the vases hold enough water to keep the flowers fresh.

When It's Your Turn for Supper Club

Make these do-ahead party dishes and spend your time with your guests.

Menu
Appetizer Cheese Tray
Curried Beef
Marinated Vegetable Tray
Dinner Rolls
Black Bottom Tarts

Appetizer Cheese Tray

   1 (11-ounce) package goat cheese
   1 tablespoon olive oil
   1 teaspoon cracked pepper
   ¼ teaspoon dried thyme
   1 Granny Smith apple, sliced
   1 Red Delicious apple, sliced
   1 cup pineapple juice
  12 slices provolone cheese
  12 slices prosciutto
   1 (10-ounce) round Gouda cheese, cut into
       16 wedges
      Garnish: fresh thyme, Champagne grapes
      French baguette, sliced and toasted

Position knife blade in food processor bowl; add first 4 ingredients. Process until smooth, stopping once to scrape sides. Spoon into a serving container; cover and chill up to 3 days.

Combine apples and pineapple juice; cover and chill. Drain before serving.

Place 1 cheese slice on top of each slice of prosciutto; roll up tightly. Place in a zip-top plastic bag, and refrigerate. Cut in half just before serving. Secure with wooden picks, if necessary.

Arrange cheese wedges, apples, prosciutto rolls, and goat cheese mixture on a large tray; garnish, if desired. Serve with bread slices. **Yield: 12 appetizer servings.**

Curried Beef

   ½ cup butter or margarine, divided
   2 medium onions, chopped
   5 pounds round steak, trimmed and cut into
       1-inch cubes
  6½ cups water, divided
   2 (10½-ounce) cans beef consommé,
       undiluted
   1 tablespoon sugar
   1 tablespoon salt
   ½ cup flaked coconut
3 to 4 tablespoons curry powder
   ½ cup all-purpose flour
   2 cups boiling water
   ½ cup currants
   6 cups hot cooked rice
      Condiments: chutney, toasted coconut,
        chopped roasted peanuts, sliced green
        onions, shredded sharp Cheddar cheese

Melt 2 tablespoons butter in a large Dutch oven. Add onion, and cook over medium-high heat, stirring constantly, until crisp-tender. Remove onion, and set aside.

Melt 1½ tablespoons butter in Dutch oven; add one-fourth of steak. Cook over medium-high heat until browned, stirring often. Drain. Repeat procedure 3 times with remaining butter and steak.

Combine beef, onion, 5½ cups water, and next 5 ingredients in Dutch oven.

Bring to a boil; cover, reduce heat, and simmer 2 hours.

Combine remaining 1 cup water and flour; stir into beef mixture, and cook until mixture thickens.

Pour 2 cups boiling water over currants; let stand 30 minutes. Drain. Stir into rice.

Serve curried beef with rice and condiments. **Yield: 12 servings.**

Hearty fare for a supper club Christmas party includes Marinated Vegetable Tray,
Curried Beef with rice and condiments, and Dinner Rolls.

Do-Ahead Party Plan

This do-ahead party plan lets you prepare for the party well in advance so that you'll have plenty of time to enjoy your guests. You can easily double the menu for a larger party. For a smaller dinner party, halve the Curried Beef.

One Month Ahead:
- Prepare and bake Dinner Rolls. Cool on a wire rack;wrap in aluminum foil, and freeze.
- Prepare and bake pastry shells for Black Bottom Tarts. Cool on a wire rack; place in an air-tight container, and freeze.

Three Days Before the Party:
- Prepare condiments for Curried Beef: toast coconut, chop peanuts, slice green onions, and shred cheese. Store separately in zip-top plastic bags; refrigerate green onions and cheese.
- Make goat cheese spread for Appetizer Cheese Tray; cover and refrigerate.
- Slice and toast French baguette. Store in an air-tight container.
- Make chocolate shavings for Black Bottom Tarts; store in a zip-top plastic bag in the refrigerator.

Day Before the Party:
- Prepare Curried Beef, and refrigerate. Soak currants as directed in boiling water; drain. Cook rice, stir in currants, and refrigerate.
- Wash garnishes for Marinated Vegetable Tray, and prepare marinated vegetables.

Day of the Party:
- Thaw Dinner Rolls.
- Make filling for Black Bottom Tarts. Thaw pastry shells, and fill. Pipe with whipped cream; garnish, if desired, and refrigerate.
- Arrange Marinated Vegetable Tray; cover and refrigerate.
- Arrange Appetizer Cheese Tray; cover and refrigerate.
- Re-heat Curried Beef in a large Dutch oven over medium-low heat, stirring occasionally until thoroughly heated.
- Open zip-top plastic bag; microwave rice at HIGH 3 minutes or until thoroughly heated.
- Bake rolls in foil at 375° for 10 to 12 minutes or until thoroughly heated.

Marinated Vegetable Tray

  1 pound small fresh green beans
  1 (16-ounce) package baby carrots
  1 (16-ounce) can small whole beets, drained
  1 (14.4-ounce) can hearts of palm, drained
    and cut in half
  1 (14-ounce) can artichoke hearts, drained
  1 pint cherry tomatoes, cut in half
1⅓ cups vegetable oil
 ½ cup white wine vinegar
  2 cloves garlic, pressed
  1 tablespoon finely chopped onion
1½ teaspoons salt
1½ teaspoons pepper
 ½ teaspoon paprika
    Garnishes: leaf lettuce, kale, purple
      cabbage, baby cauliflower

Arrange green beans in a steamer basket and place over boiling water. Cover and steam 10 minutes or until crisp-tender. Remove from steamer, and plunge into ice water; drain. Set aside.

Cook carrots in boiling salted water to cover 7 to 10 minutes or until crisp-tender. Drain.

Place green beans, carrots, and each of the next 4 vegetables separately into heavy-duty, zip-top plastic bags or shallow containers. Set aside.

Combine oil and next 6 ingredients in a jar. Cover tightly, and shake vigorously. Pour over vegetables, tossing well. Seal bags or cover; refrigerate 8 hours, turning vegetables once. Drain and arrange on a lettuce-lined tray. Garnish, if desired. **Yield: 8 servings.**

Dinner Rolls

    ⅓ cup shortening
    1 cup water, divided
    1 package active dry yeast
    ¼ cup warm water (105° to 115°)
    1 large egg
    ⅓ cup sugar
    1 teaspoon salt
3¼ to 3¾ cups all-purpose flour
    2 tablespoons butter or margarine, melted

Combine shortening and ½ cup water in a small saucepan; heat until shortening melts. Cool to 105° to 115°.

    Combine yeast and ¼ cup warm water in a 1-cup liquid measuring cup; let stand 5 minutes.

    Combine egg, sugar, and salt in a large mixing bowl. Stir in remaining ½ cup water, shortening mixture, and yeast mixture. Gradually stir in enough flour to make a stiff dough.

    Turn dough out onto a heavily floured surface, and knead until smooth and elastic (about 5 minutes). Place in a well-greased bowl, turning to grease top. Cover and refrigerate 8 hours.

    Punch dough down; turn out onto a floured surface, and knead 4 or 5 times. Roll out to ¼-inch thickness.

    Cut with a 2½-inch round cutter. Make a crease with the dull edge of a knife just off center on each round; brush with butter. Fold larger side over smaller so edges will meet; press gently to seal. Repeat procedure with remaining dough. Place rolls in a lightly greased 13- x 9- x 2-inch pan. Cover and let rise in a warm place (85°), free from drafts, 1 hour or until doubled in bulk.

    Bake at 400° for 16 to 18 minutes or until golden brown. **Yield: 21 rolls.**

Black Bottom Tarts

    1 (15-ounce) package refrigerated piecrusts
    1 (3-ounce) package vanilla pudding mix
    2 cups milk
    1 cup semisweet chocolate morsels
    1 tablespoon rum *
    1 cup whipping cream, whipped
        Garnish: chocolate shavings

Unfold each pastry, and roll to ⅛-inch thickness on a lightly floured surface; using a 2½-inch round cutter, cut

The proof is in the pudding – rum- and chocolate-flavored pudding, to be exact. Allow two or three of these bite-size Black Bottom Tarts per guest.

out 24 circles. Place circles in ungreased miniature (1¾-inch) muffin pans. Prick pastry with a fork.

    Bake at 425° for 4 to 5 minutes or until lightly browned. Cool in pans on wire racks.

    Combine pudding mix and milk, and cook pudding according to package directions for pie filling. Remove ½ cup hot pudding; add chocolate morsels, stirring until smooth. Spoon 1 teaspoon into each pastry.

    Stir rum into remaining pudding. Spoon evenly over chocolate mixture. Chill 2 hours.

    Pipe or dollop with whipped cream; garnish, if desired. **Yield: 4 dozen.**

*1 teaspoon rum extract may be substituted.

Note: For a 9-inch pie, spoon chocolate mixture into baked 9-inch pastry shell; top with rum-flavored pudding. Dollop with whipped cream, and garnish, if desired.

Get a jump on your Christmas list with Herbed Vinegar and Cranberry Spice Vinegar, which you can make months ahead. Present them in decorative bottles stopped with custom-crafted corks (see box at right).

Gifts from the Kitchen

From quick-to-fix bean soup mix to scrumptious scones, you'll find something here to please every palate.

Herbed Vinegar

    1 bunch fresh parsley
10 to 12 fresh jalapeño peppers, cut in half
      lengthwise
10 to 12 large cloves garlic, cut in half lengthwise
    1 large sweet red pepper, cut into strips
    1 large green pepper, cut into strips
    1 lemon, sliced
    2 (17-ounce) bottles white wine vinegar
      Additional parsley sprigs, jalapeño peppers,
       garlic cloves, pepper strips, lemon slices
      (optional)

Place first 6 ingredients in a large glass container.

    Bring vinegar to a boil, and pour over parsley mixture. Cover and store at room temperature 2 weeks.

    Pour vinegar mixture through a large wire-mesh strainer into bottles, discarding solids. If desired, add additional parsley sprigs, jalapeño peppers, garlic cloves, pepper strips, and lemon slices. **Yield: 5 cups.**

Cranberry Spice Vinegar

    3 (17-ounce) bottles white wine vinegar
    1 cup cranberry juice
  ½ cup sugar
    3 (3-inch) sticks cinnamon
    1 (1.6-ounce) jar whole cloves
    1 large orange, sliced
      Additional orange slices, whole cloves,
       cinnamon sticks (optional)

Combine first 3 ingredients in a large nonaluminum saucepan.

    Bring to a boil.

    Place cinnamon and remaining ingredients in a large glass container. Pour vinegar mixture over spices. Cover and store at room temperature 2 weeks.

Bottle Stoppers with Style

The beads on these bottle stoppers came from a Parisian department store and may be hard to find in this country, but you can adapt the basic idea and use materials that you have on hand. Costume necklaces that have come unstrung or that you no longer wear may offer large metal or polished beads. Check crafts stores for large wooden, metal, or glass beads. Or make your own beads, using polymer clay.

    Use wine corks or purchased corks to fit the mouth of your bottle.

    Drill a hole into the cork, being careful not to go all the way through. Choose a drill bit to suit the size of the copper wire – the wire in the photograph is No. 4, available from a hardware store. Be sure the wire will fit through the holes in your beads.

    Put a drop of Super Glue into the hole in the cork and insert the wire. After the glue dries, slide on a flat bead and then coil the wire as desired, using pliers for leverage. Slip on beads as desired. Cut the copper wire about ⅜ inch above the last bead. To cover the wire and make a finial, put a drop of Super Glue just above the bead, attach the end of a length of gold craft wire, and wrap the gold wire tightly around the end of the copper wire.

    Pour vinegar mixture through a large wire-mesh strainer into decorative bottles, discarding solids. If desired, add additional orange slices, whole cloves, and cinnamon sticks to filled bottles. **Yield: 7 cups.**

Poppy Seed Dressing

Make this dressing ahead and present it with a fruit basket.

> 1 (6-ounce) can frozen limeade, thawed and
>   undiluted
> ½ cup honey
> ¼ teaspoon salt
> ¾ cup vegetable oil
> 2 teaspoons poppy seeds

Combine first 3 ingredients in container of an electric blender; process 20 seconds. With blender on high, gradually add oil in a slow steady stream. Stir in poppy seeds. Pour mixture into a bottle; refrigerate up to 1 month. **Yield: 2 cups.**

Directions for gift card: Store Poppy Seed Dressing in refrigerator up to 1 month.

Pumpkin-Mincemeat Bread

> 3½ cups all-purpose flour
> 2 teaspoons baking soda
> 1½ teaspoons salt
> 1½ cups sugar
> 1½ cups firmly packed brown sugar
> 2 tablespoons pumpkin pie spice
> 4 large eggs
> ⅔ cup water
> 1 (16-ounce) can pumpkin (2 cups)
> 1 cup vegetable oil
> 1½ cups prepared mincemeat
> 1 cup chopped pecans

Combine first 6 ingredients in a large bowl; make a well in center of mixture.

Combine eggs and next 3 ingredients; add to flour mixture, stirring just until moistened. Stir in mincement and pecans. Spoon batter into 3 greased 8½- x 4½- x 3-inch loafpans.

Bake at 350° for 1 hour or until a wooden pick inserted in center comes out clean. Cool in pans on wire racks 10 minutes; remove from pans, and let cool on wire racks. **Yield: 3 loaves.**

Pickled Vegetables

> 1 large head cauliflower
> 2 quarts water
> 1 quart white vinegar
> ¾ cup honey
> 3 tablespoons mustard seeds
> 1½ teaspoons celery seeds
> ½ teaspoon black peppercorns
> 1 pound baby carrots, scraped
> 6 celery stalks, cut into thin 2-inch strips
> 1 medium-size green pepper, cut into thin,
>   1½-inch strips
> 1 medium-size sweet red pepper, cut into
>   thin, 1½-inch strips
> 1 (16-ounce) can whole green beans, drained
> 8 small cloves garlic
> 8 small hot peppers
> 1 teaspoon salt

Remove large outer leaves of cauliflower; break into flowerets. Set aside.

Combine water and next 5 ingredients in a nonaluminum Dutch oven. Bring to a boil; reduce heat, and simmer 30 minutes.

Remove foam from surface. Add carrots. Bring to a boil; reduce heat, and simmer 3 minutes. Add cauliflower and celery. Bring to a boil; reduce heat, and simmer 5 minutes.

Add pepper strips and green beans, and simmer 3 minutes.

Spoon vegetables into 8 (2-cup) containers. Pour hot vinegar mixture over vegetables, evenly distributing spices.

Add 1 clove garlic, 1 hot pepper, and ⅛ teaspoon salt to each container. Let cool.

Seal containers, and refrigerate 1 week. **Yield: 8 (2-cup) gifts.**

Directions for gift card: Store Pickled Vegetables in refrigerator up to 3 weeks.

Jars of Pickled Vegetables are so pretty you won't want to wrap them. Just cover the lid with a square of handmade paper and tie with a gold ribbon.

Assemble Bean-Pasta Soup Mix months ahead or put it together at the last minute.

Bean-Pasta Soup Mix

- ³⁄₄ cup dried onion flakes
- 2 (¹⁄₂-ounce) jars dried celery flakes
- ¹⁄₂ cup dried parsley flakes
- 3 tablespoons dried basil
- 3 tablespoons dried oregano
- 2 teaspoons garlic powder
- 2 teaspoons coarsely ground pepper
- 2 (2¹⁄₄-ounce) jars beef-flavored bouillon granules
- 1 (16-ounce) package dried black-eyed peas
- 1 (16-ounce) package dried black beans
- 1 (16-ounce) package dried kidney beans
- 1 (16-ounce) package dried navy beans
- 1 (16-ounce) package small shell pasta, uncooked

Combine first 7 ingredients; divide evenly, and place in 6 airtight plastic bags. Add 2 tablespoons plus ¹⁄₄ teaspoon bouillon granules to each package. Label "Herb Mix" and seal.

Combine black-eyed peas and next 3 ingredients; divide evenly and place in 6 airtight plastic bags. Label "Bean Mix" and seal.

Place ¹⁄₃ cup pasta into 6 airtight plastic bags. Label "Pasta" and seal.

Place 1 bag herb mix, 1 bag bean mix, and 1 bag pasta in a gift container; repeat procedure with remaining bags. **Yield: 6 (3-bag) gifts.**

Directions for gift recipe card: Sort and wash bean mix; place in a Dutch oven. Cover with water 2 inches above beans; soak 8 hours. Drain.

Combine beans, 3 quarts water, herb mix, 1 carrot, chopped, and ²⁄₃ cup chopped cooked ham in Dutch oven. Bring to a boil; reduce heat, and simmer 2½ hours, stirring occasionally.

Add 1 (14½-ounce) can Mexican-style stewed tomatoes, undrained, and pasta; cook 20 minutes. **Yield: 9 cups.**

Note: To use the quick-soak method, place beans in a Dutch oven; cover with water 2 inches above beans. Bring to a boil. Remove from heat; cover, and let stand 1 hour. Drain.

Applesauce-Spice Pound Cake

      1 cup butter or margarine, softened
   1½ cups firmly packed brown sugar
   1½ cups sugar
      5 large eggs
   1½ cups applesauce
      2 teaspoons baking soda
      3 cups all-purpose flour, divided
      1 teaspoon ground cinnamon
      1 teaspoon ground nutmeg
    ½ teaspoon ground cloves
    ½ teaspoon ground allspice
   1½ cups raisins
      1 cup chopped pecans

Beat butter at medium speed with an electric mixer about 2 minutes or until soft and creamy. Gradually add sugars, beating at medium speed 5 to 7 minutes. Add eggs, 1 at a time, beating just until yellow disappears.

Combine applesauce and baking soda; set aside.

Combine 2¾ cups flour and spices; add to butter mixture alternately with applesauce mixture, beginning and ending with flour mixture. Mix at low speed just until blended after each addition.

Combine remaining ¼ cup flour, raisins, and pecans; fold into batter. Pour batter into a greased and floured 12-cup Bundt pan.

Bake at 325° for 1 hour and 15 to 20 minutes or until a wooden pick inserted in center comes out clean. Cool in pan on a wire rack 10 to 15 minutes; remove from pan, and let cool completely on a wire rack. **Yield: 1 (10-inch) cake.**

Ginger Dressing

    ⅓ cup vegetable oil
    ⅓ cup reduced-sodium soy sauce
    ⅓ cup white vinegar
      1 teaspoon ground ginger
      1 teaspoon garlic powder
         Dash of pepper

Combine all ingredients in a jar. Cover tightly, and shake vigorously. Pour into a bottle; refrigerate up to 1 month. **Yield: about 1 cup.**

Directions for gift card: Store Ginger Dressing in refrigerator up to 1 month. Serve as a salad dressing or use as a marinade for pork.

St. Nicholas Day Cake

Celebrate the saint's day on December 6 with this almond- and cinnamon-flavored streusel cake.

      1 (27.25-ounce) package cinnamon streusel
         cake mix
      3 large eggs
    ¾ cup water
    ⅓ cup vegetable oil
      2 teaspoons ground cardamom *
    ¾ teaspoon almond extract, divided
    ¼ cup chopped almonds, toasted
2 to 3 teaspoons water

Combine cake mix, next four ingredients, and ½ teaspoon almond extract. Beat at low speed with an electric mixer until ingredients are moistened. Beat at medium speed 2 minutes. Spoon three-fourths of batter into a greased and floured 10-inch tube pan. Set aside.

Combine streusel mix packet and almonds; sprinkle ¾ cup mixture over batter. Top with remaining batter and sprinkle with remaining streusel mixture.

Bake at 350° for 55 minutes or until a wooden pick inserted in center comes out clean. Cool in pan on a wire rack 30 minutes; remove from pan.

Combine glaze packet, 2 to 3 teaspoons water, and remaining ¼ teaspoon almond extract; drizzle over warm cake. **Yield: 1 (10-inch) cake.**

Note: 1 teaspoon ground ginger may be substituted.

Boursin Cheese Spread

Fill a crock with this creamy, herbed cheese spread and package it in a basket with fruit, a loaf of French bread, and a bottle of wine – an instant party!

    2 (16-ounce) packages cream cheese, softened
    1 (8-ounce) carton whipped butter
    2 cloves garlic, pressed
    ½ teaspoon dried oregano
    ¼ teaspoon dried basil
    ¼ teaspoon dried marjoram
    ¼ teaspoon dried thyme
    ¼ teaspoon pepper

Beat cream cheese at medium speed with an electric mixer until smooth; add butter and remaining ingredients, mixing until blended. Spoon into airtight containers. Store in refrigerator up to 1 week. **Yield: 3½ cups.**

Directions for gift card: Store Boursin Cheese Spread in refrigerator up to 1 week. Let stand at room temperature 30 minutes before serving. Serve with crackers or French bread.

Quick Crackers

These are wonderful as a snack or served with a salad.

    1 (16-ounce) package egg roll wrappers
      Vegetable cooking spray
    3 tablespoons olive oil
    3 tablespoons water
    ¾ teaspoon garlic salt
    ¾ teaspoon Italian seasoning
    ¼ to ½ teaspoon ground red pepper
      Parmesan cheese

Cut each egg roll wrapper into 4 strips with kitchen shears. Arrange in a single layer on baking sheets coated with cooking spray. Set aside.

Combine olive oil and next 4 ingredients. Brush mixture on each strip.

Bake at 375° for 5 to 6 minutes or until golden.

Sprinkle lightly with Parmesan cheese. Remove to wire racks to cool. Store in an airtight container. **Yield: 6 dozen.**

Pear Honey

A jar of Pear Honey is a welcome gift by itself, or an excellent partner for homemade bread.

    3 large pears, peeled, cored, and quartered
      (1½ pounds)
    1 (8-ounce) can crushed pineapple, drained
    1 tablespoon grated lemon rind
    2 tablespoons lemon juice
    4 cups sugar

Position knife blade in food processor bowl; add pears. Process until finely chopped. Do not puree. Measure pears to equal 4 cups.

Combine 4 cups pears, pineapple, and remaining ingredients in a heavy saucepan; bring slowly to a boil. Cook, stirring frequently, until sugar dissolves. Reduce heat, and simmer, stirring frequently, 40 minutes or until thick.

Spoon mixture into hot sterilized jars, filling to ¼-inch from top; wipe jar rims. Cover at once with metal lids, and screw on bands. Process in boiling-water bath 5 minutes. Cool on a wire rack. Store in a cool, dark place. **Yield: 3 half pints.**

Directions for gift card: After opening, keep Pear Honey refrigerated.

Yogurt-Praline Candy

      Butter-flavored cooking spray
    1 cup firmly packed brown sugar
    ½ cup sugar
    ½ cup nonfat plain yogurt
    2 cups walnut or pecan halves
    1 teaspoon vanilla extract

Coat wax paper with cooking spray; set aside.

Combine sugars and yogurt in a medium saucepan. Bring to a boil over medium heat. (Do not stir.) Boil 2 to 3 minutes or until a candy thermometer reads 232°.

Remove from heat; stir in walnuts and vanilla.

Spoon mixture evenly onto prepared wax paper; let stand until firm. Break into small pieces. Store in an airtight container. **Yield: 1½ pounds.**

Please your sweet-toothed friends with Hot Raisin Scones, Pear Honey, or Yogurt-Praline Candy. Package the candy in cardboard containers covered with strips of colored tissue paper applied and sealed with Mod Podge®. (If you stuff extra tissue paper inside the container, be sure it's the kind that won't fade or bleed color onto the food.)

Hot Raisin Scones

These were very popular in the *Southern Living* Test Kitchens. The ingredients are simple and inexpensive, and the results are impressively tasty. Wrap them up for a favorite aunt and give her a box of flavored tea to accompany them.

   2 cups all-purpose flour
   2 teaspoons baking powder
   ½ teaspoon baking soda
   ¼ teaspoon salt
   2 tablespoons sugar
   1 teaspoon grated lemon rind
   ½ cup cold butter or margarine
   ½ cup raisins
   ¾ cup buttermilk

Combine first 6 ingredients; cut in butter with a pastry blender until mixture is crumbly. Add raisins, tossing lightly. Add buttermilk, stirring until dry ingredients are moistened.

Turn dough out onto a lightly floured surface, and knead lightly 6 times. Divide dough in half. Shape each portion into a 7-inch circle on an ungreased cookie sheet; cut each circle into 6 wedges. Bake at 425° for 10 minutes. Cool on wire racks.

Place scones on 2 (8-inch) cake boards; wrap with heavy-duty plastic wrap. Freeze up to 1 month. **Yield: 6 scones.**

Directions for gift card: Thaw scone at room temperature; bake at 425° for 6 to 7 minutes or until thoroughly heated.

TO: BOB
FROM: TINA

Gifts Kids Can Make

Start your holidays with giggles galore – have a children's day in the kitchen.

People Chow

This recipe was sent in by a young *Southern Living* reader. She thought the candy looked a lot like Puppy Chow – but this is very definitely people food! It was a big hit with the Test Kitchens home economists, who liked the flavor combination of graham cereal, chocolate, and peanut butter.

    ½ cup butter or margarine
    1 cup creamy peanut butter
    1 (11½-ounce) package milk chocolate
         morsels
    1 (12-ounce) box honey graham cereal
    3 cups sifted powdered sugar

Combine first 3 ingredients in a large saucepan; cook over low heat, stirring constantly, until chocolate melts and mixture is smooth.

Add cereal, stirring to coat.

Place half of the powdered sugar in a large heavy-duty, zip-top plastic bag; add cereal mixture and remaining half of powdered sugar. Seal bag, and gently shake to coat.

Pour mixture onto 2 cookie sheets; let dry. Separate large pieces with fork, if necessary. **Yield: 12 cups.**

Easy Reindeer Cookies

    1 (20-ounce) package refrigerated sliceable
         peanut butter cookie dough
    60 (2-inch) pretzel twists
    60 semisweet chocolate morsels
    30 red candy-coated chocolate pieces

Easy Reindeer Cookies will be the hit of your child's class party. For teachers and friends, make batches of People Chow. Package each gift in a quart-size paint can (you can buy new ones from paint stores). Photocopy the label on page 159, let your child color it as desired, and apply it to the can with spray adhesive.

Freeze dough 15 minutes.

Cut dough into 30 (¼-inch-thick) slices. Place 4 inches apart on ungreased cookie sheets. Using thumb and forefinger, pinch in each slice about two-thirds of the way down to shape face.

Press a pretzel on each side of larger end for antlers.

Press in chocolate morsels for eyes.

Bake at 350° for 9 to 11 minutes or until lightly browned.

Remove from oven, and press in red candy for nose. Let stand 2 minutes; remove to wire racks to cool. **Yield: 2½ dozen.**

Colorful Christmas Balls

    2½ cups graham cracker crumbs
    1 cup sifted powdered sugar
    ½ cup finely chopped pecans
    ½ cup candy-coated chocolate mini-morsels
    1 cup flaked coconut (optional)
    1 cup chocolate syrup
    1½ teaspoons vanilla extract
    10 (2-ounce) squares vanilla-flavored candy
         coating
        Assorted nonpareils

Combine first 4 ingredients in a large bowl; add coconut, if desired. Stir in syrup and vanilla.

Shape into 1-inch balls, and chill 1 hour.

Place candy coating in top of a double boiler; bring water to a boil. Reduce heat to low; cook until coating melts. Remove from heat.

Dip each ball into candy coating; place on wax paper. Sprinkle with nonpareils. **Yield: 5 dozen.**

Christmas Popcorn

This recipe was submitted by a child and would be a tasty gift to give a child, but the actual preparation should be done by an adult.

   1 cup butter or margarine
  ¾ cup sugar
   1 (3-ounce) package cherry-flavored gelatin
   3 tablespoons water
   1 tablespoon light corn syrup
10 cups popped popcorn

Combine first 5 ingredients in a heavy 2-quart saucepan; bring to a boil over medium heat, stirring constantly.

Cook, stirring occasionally, until a candy thermometer reads 255°.

Place popcorn in a large bowl; pour hot mixture over popcorn, and stir until thoroughly coated. Spoon into a large roaster or baking pan.

Bake at 300° for 10 minutes, stirring twice. Transfer to lightly greased aluminum foil; cool and break into clusters. **Yield: 5 cups.**

Zebra Cookies

1½ cups butter, softened
  2 cups sugar
  1 large egg
  ½ cup orange juice
  1 teaspoon vanilla extract
3½ cups all-purpose flour
   Vegetable cooking spray
84 foil-wrapped solid white chocolate and milk
    chocolate pieces, unwrapped*

Beat butter at medium speed with an electric mixer until creamy; gradually add sugar, beating well. Add egg, beating until blended.

Stir in orange juice and vanilla. Gradually add flour, beating well. Cover and chill.

Shape dough into 1-inch balls.

Place paper baking cups in miniature (1¾-inch) muffin pans, and coat with cooking spray. Place dough balls into baking cups.

Bake at 400° for 12 minutes.

Remove from oven, and immediately press a chocolate piece into center of each cookie; let cool. Store in airtight containers. **Yield: 7 dozen.**

*For foil-wrapped solid white chocolate and milk chocolate pieces, we used Hershey's Hugs.

Gingerbread Frames

An adult will need to make the gingerbread and cut the frame shapes, but children as young as four years old can decorate and assemble the frames.

Make a template by cutting a piece of cardboard into a 5-inch x 7-inch rectangle. Center and cut an opening 2¾ inches x 4¾ inches for the picture. The dough is edible, so you can bake any scraps left over from making the frames.

  1 cup firmly packed brown sugar
  ¾ cup sugar
  ¾ cup honey
  ¼ cup butter or margarine
  ⅓ cup lemon juice
  6 cups all-purpose flour
  ¼ cup baking powder
  ¼ teaspoon salt
  2 teaspoons ground ginger
  1 teaspoon ground cinnamon
  ½ teaspoon ground cloves
  ½ teaspoon ground allspice
  2 large eggs
   Red or green paste food coloring (optional)
   Decorator Frosting
24 (4-inch) peppermint sticks
   Assorted candies
16 (6-inch) candy canes

Combine first 4 ingredients in a medium saucepan; bring to a boil, stirring until sugar melts. Remove from heat; stir in lemon juice. Pour into a large bowl, and cool to room temperature.

Combine flour and next 6 ingredients. Stir 2 cups flour mixture and eggs into sugar mixture. Gradually add remaining flour mixture, mixing well. (Dough will appear dry.) Shape dough into a ball; knead on a floured surface until smooth, adding paste food coloring, if desired.

Roll half of dough to ¼-inch thickness on a lightly greased cookie sheet. (Placing a damp towel under cookie sheet will keep it from slipping as you roll.) Using template, cut out 1 frame front (with opening) and 1 back; remove excess dough and set aside.

Bake frame pieces at 325° for 15 minutes or until firm. Loosen gingerbread with a spatula, and let cool 1 minute on cookie sheet. Remove to wire racks to cool completely. Repeat procedure with remaining dough.

To assemble frames: Spoon Decorator Frosting into a decorating bag or a heavy-duty, zip-top plastic bag; snip off end or small corner of zip-top bag. On the back of each cutout frame, pipe frosting on 3 sides. (Leave 1 side open for inserting photograph.) Push 3 peppermint sticks into frosting. Pipe frosting on top of peppermint sticks, and attach solid frame back. Let dry.

Decorate frames with frosting and assorted candies, as desired. Let dry.

To make stand: Carefully attach 2 candy canes to back of each frame with frosting. Let dry before standing. **Yield: 8 frames.**

Decorator Frosting:

 2 **cups sifted powdered sugar**
1½ **tablespoons meringue powder**
 3 **tablespoons water**

Combine all ingredients in a mixing bowl; beat at high speed with an electric mixer 10 minutes or until stiff peaks form. Cover with a damp cloth to prevent drying. **Yield: 1½ cups.**

Grownups will need to make the dough and cut the shapes for Gingerbread Frames, but the decoration is pure kids' stuff. For frame assembly, see below.

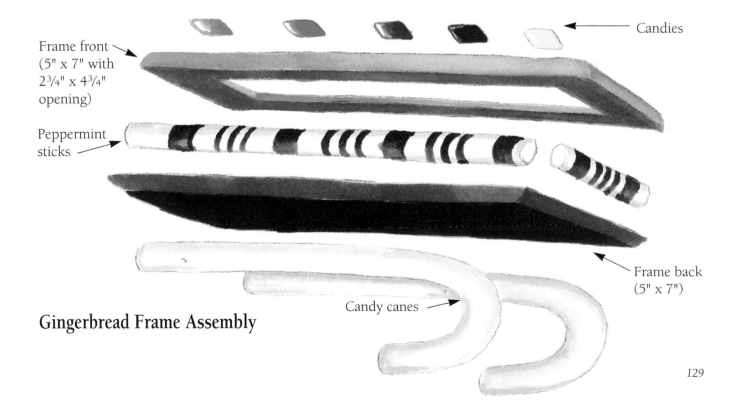

Candies

Frame front (5" x 7" with 2¾" x 4¾" opening)

Peppermint sticks

Frame back (5" x 7")

Candy canes

Gingerbread Frame Assembly

Give Your Meal a Happy Ending

These luscious desserts will satisfy any sweet tooth.

Triple Chocolate Terrine

    3 cups whipping cream, divided
    7 ounces bittersweet chocolate,
      chopped
    1 cup milk chocolate morsels
    4 ounces white chocolate, chopped
    1 (4-inch) vanilla bean, split
      Chocolate Fudge Sauce
      Raspberry Sauce
      Garnishes: fresh mint leaves, fresh or
        frozen raspberries

Heat cream in a heavy saucepan over medium heat until very hot (do not boil). Remove from heat.

Pour 1¼ cups hot cream into a bowl; add bittersweet chocolate, stirring until smooth. Set aside.

Pour 1 cup hot cream into a bowl; add milk chocolate, stirring until smooth. Set aside.

Pour remaining ¾ cup hot cream into a bowl; add white chocolate, stirring until smooth. Set aside.

Scrape pulp from vanilla bean, discarding bean; stir pulp into white chocolate mixture.

Cover each bowl; refrigerate 3 hours to chill mixture.

Line an 8½- x 4½- x 3-inch loafpan with aluminum foil, allowing foil to overlap sides of pan; set aside.

Beat white chocolate mixture at high speed with an electric mixer until soft peaks form (do not overbeat). Spoon into prepared pan; set aside.

Beat milk chocolate mixture at high speed with an electric mixer until soft peaks form (do not overbeat). Spoon over white chocolate mixture; set aside.

Beat bittersweet chocolate mixture at high speed with an electric mixer until soft peaks form (do not overbeat). Spoon over milk chocolate mixture.

Cover and refrigerate 8 hours.

Lift terrine using aluminum foil; remove foil, and smooth surface with a knife. (Terrine will be soft.) Cut into 8 slices.

Spoon Chocolate Fudge Sauce and Raspberry Sauce onto individual plates; place a slice of terrine on sauces. Garnish, if desired. **Yield: 8 servings.**

Chocolate Fudge Sauce:

    1 cup semisweet chocolate morsels
    1 tablespoon butter or margarine
    ½ teaspoon vanilla extract
    ¾ cup whipping cream

Combine chocolate morsels and butter in a heavy saucepan; place over medium-low heat, and cook, stirring constantly, until chocolate melts.

Stir in vanilla; gradually add whipping cream, stirring until smooth. Cook, stirring constantly, about 5 minutes. Remove from heat, and cool. **Yield: about 1⅓ cups.**

Raspberry Sauce:

    1 (10-ounce) package frozen raspberries,
      thawed and undrained
    1 tablespoon cornstarch
    1 tablespoon light corn syrup

Place raspberries in a wire-mesh strainer; press with back of a spoon against the sides of the strainer to squeeze out juice. Discard pulp and seeds remaining in strainer.

Combine raspberry juice, cornstarch, and corn syrup in a small saucepan; place over medium heat, stirring constantly, until mixture comes to a boil. Boil 1 minute, stirring constantly. Remove from heat, and cool. Chill. **Yield: ½ cup.**

Triple Chocolate Terrine combines four great flavors – raspberry and three kinds of chocolate – in a creamy, light-tasting dessert.

Coeur à la Crème

1½ cups small curd cottage cheese
2 (8-ounce) packages cream cheese, softened
½ cup sour cream
3 tablespoons powdered sugar
⅓ cup whipping cream, whipped
   Raspberry Aspic
   Garnishes: fresh or frozen raspberries,
     fresh mint

Combine first 4 ingredients in a mixing bowl; beat at medium speed with an electric mixer until smooth.

Fold in whipped cream.

Line a 4-cup heart mold with cheesecloth, letting cloth hang over edges. Spoon mixture into prepared pan. Fold cheesecloth over top.

Cover and chill 8 hours.

Unmold onto a serving platter. Place Raspberry Aspic around mold, and garnish, if desired. Serve with short-bread cookies or gingersnaps. **Yield: 25 appetizer-size servings.**

Raspberry Aspic:

1 envelope unflavored gelatin
⅓ cup cold water
2 tablespoons sugar
⅓ cup cranberry juice cocktail
1 (10-ounce) package frozen raspberries, thawed

Sprinkle gelatin over cold water in a small saucepan; let stand 1 minute.

Add sugar, and cook over low heat, stirring until gelatin dissolves (about 2 minutes). Remove from heat.

Stir in cranberry juice. Set aside.

Place raspberries in container of an electric blender; process until smooth. Pour through a wire-mesh strainer into a small bowl, discarding seeds.

Stir raspberry juice into gelatin mixture. Pour into a lightly greased 8-inch square dish.

Cover and chill 8 hours. Unmold and cut into small squares. **Yield: 1½ cups.**

Grand Marnier Soufflé

1 tablespoon butter or margarine
2 tablespoons sugar
8 large eggs, separated
⅔ cup sugar
⅓ cup Grand Marnier
⅓ cup frozen orange juice concentrate,
   thawed and undiluted
1 teaspoon grated orange rind
   Powdered sugar

Cut a piece of aluminum foil long enough to fit around a 2½-quart soufflé dish, allowing a 1-inch overlap; fold foil lengthwise into thirds. Lightly butter one side of foil and bottom of dish. Wrap foil around outside of dish, buttered side against dish, allowing it to extend 3 inches above rim to form a collar. Secure with freezer tape.

Sprinkle dish with 2 tablespoons sugar, tilting dish to discard excess sugar. Set aside.

Beat egg yolks in top of a double boiler with a hand-held portable mixer; gradually add ⅔ cup sugar, beating until mixture is thick and pale.

Bring water to a boil. Reduce heat to low, and beat at high speed until mixture thickens (about 10 minutes).

Stir in Grand Marnier, orange juice concentrate, and orange rind.

Cover and chill until cool, or if desired, up to 8 hours.

Beat egg whites until stiff peaks form; gently fold into egg yolk mixture. Pour into prepared dish.

Bake at 375° for 20 to 25 minutes or until puffed and lightly browned (center will be slightly soft).

Sprinkle with powdered sugar. Serve immediately. **Yield: 6 servings.**

Ripple Currant Cake

1 cup finely chopped pecans, divided
2 cups sugar, divided
1½ tablespoons cocoa
1 tablespoon ground cinnamon
1 cup butter or margarine, softened
1 (8-ounce) package cream cheese, softened
4 large eggs
1½ teaspoons vanilla extract
2¼ cups all-purpose flour
1½ teaspoons baking powder
½ cup currants or raisins

Sprinkle ½ cup pecans into a greased and floured 12-cup Bundt pan; set aside.

Combine ½ cup sugar, cocoa, and cinnamon; set aside.

Beat butter and cream cheese at medium speed with an electric mixer about 2 minutes or until creamy. Gradually add remaining 1½ cups sugar, beating at medium speed 5 to 7 minutes. Add eggs, 1 at a time, beating just until yellow disappears. Stir in vanilla.

Combine flour and baking powder; add to butter mixture, beating just until blended. Stir in currants and remaining ½ cup pecans.

Spoon one-third of batter into prepared pan; sprinkle with half of sugar mixture. Repeat procedure, ending with batter.

Bake at 325° for 1 hour and 5 minutes or until a wooden pick inserted in center comes out clean.

Cool in pan on a wire rack 10 to 15 minutes; remove from pan, and cool completely on a wire rack. **Yield: 1 (10-inch) cake.**

Raisin-Walnut Pie

¼ cup butter or margarine, softened
¾ cup firmly packed brown sugar
3 large eggs, lightly beaten
1 cup dark corn syrup
1 teaspoon vanilla extract
1 cup raisins
½ cup finely chopped English or black walnuts
½ (15-ounce) package refrigerated piecrusts
1 teaspoon all-purpose flour

Combine first 3 ingredients in a medium bowl; beat at medium speed with an electric mixer until blended. Add corn syrup and vanilla, mixing well. Stir in raisins and walnuts. Set aside.

Unfold piecrust, and press out fold lines; sprinkle with flour, spreading over surface. Place crust, floured side down, in a 9-inch pieplate. Fold edges under and crimp.

Spoon in filling.

Bake at 375° for 50 minutes or until firm, covering loosely with aluminum foil after 30 minutes. **Yield: 1 (9-inch) pie.**

Cranberry Pie

1 (15-ounce) package refrigerated piecrusts
1 teaspoon all-purpose flour
1 (12-ounce) package cranberries
½ cup raisins
1½ cups sugar
¼ cup all-purpose flour
¼ cup light corn syrup
⅔ cup chopped walnuts
½ teaspoon grated orange rind
1 tablespoon orange juice

Unfold 1 piecrust, and press out fold lines; sprinkle with 1 teaspoon flour. Invert crust, and place floured side down in a 9-inch pieplate. Set aside.

Position knife blade in food processor bowl; add half of cranberries and half of raisins. Pulse 8 to 10 times or until chopped, stopping occasionally to scrape down sides. Transfer mixture to a large bowl. Repeat procedure with remaining cranberries and raisins. Stir in sugar and remaining ingredients; spoon into piecrust.

Roll out remaining piecrust on a lightly floured surface to remove fold lines; cut into ½-inch strips, and arrange in a lattice design over filling. Fold edges under and flute.

Bake at 350° for 30 minutes.

Cover pastry edges with aluminum foil, and bake 20 to 25 additional minutes or until golden. Cool on a wire rack. **Yield: 1 (9-inch) pie.**

Triple Chocolate Mint-Cream Layer Cake

This cake is a hostess's dream: it's gorgeous, it's delicious, and you can freeze it before or after icing it.

     3 (1-ounce) squares unsweetened chocolate
    ½ cup butter or margarine, softened
    1⅓ cups sugar
     2 large eggs
    1⅓ cups cake flour
     1 teaspoon baking soda
    ¼ teaspoon salt
    ⅔ cup milk
     1 teaspoon vanilla extract
       Mint-Cream Filling
       Chocolate Filling
       Rich Chocolate Frosting
       Garnishes: chocolaty-mint thin triangles and
         shavings

Grease 3 (8-inch) round cakepans; line with wax paper, and grease and flour wax paper. Set aside.

Melt chocolate squares in a heavy saucepan over low heat, stirring occasionally. Set aside.

Beat butter at medium speed with an electric mixer until creamy; gradually add sugar, beating well. Add eggs, 1 at a time, beating after each addition. Stir in melted chocolate.

Combine flour, baking soda, and salt; add to chocolate mixture alternately with milk, beginning and ending with flour mixture. Stir in vanilla. Spoon batter into prepared pans.

Bake at 350° for 25 minutes or until a wooden pick inserted in center comes out clean. Cool in pans on wire racks 10 minutes; remove from pans, and cool completely on wire racks.

Stack layers, rotating each one until cake is level; cut a ¼-inch V-shaped notch in side of cake to use as a guide in assembling cake. (See photo 1, next page.)

Cut each layer horizontally into 2 layers. (See photo 2, next page.) Place 1 layer on an 8-inch cardboard round. Spread with one-third of Mint-Cream Filling; top with

second layer, lining up notches, and spread with half of Chocolate Filling. Top with third layer. Repeat layering, ending with sixth cake layer. (See photo 3, next page.) Wrap and freeze up to 1 month, if desired.

Frost top and sides of cake with Rich Chocolate Frosting, reserving 1 cup frosting. Pipe rosettes around top edge of cake with reserved frosting. Garnish, if desired. **Yield: 1 (8-inch) cake.**

Mint-Cream Filling:

    1¾ cups whipping cream
     10 drops liquid green food coloring
     ¼ cup sifted powdered sugar
     ¼ teaspoon peppermint extract

Combine whipping cream and food coloring; beat at medium speed with an electric mixer until foamy. Gradually add powdered sugar, beating until soft peaks form. Stir in extract. **Yield: 3 cups.**

Chocolate Filling:

     1 cup semisweet chocolate morsels
     ¼ cup butter or margarine
     ½ cup whipping cream
     ¼ cup sugar

Combine all ingredients in a heavy saucepan. Cook over low heat, stirring constantly, until mixture is smooth.

Place saucepan in a bowl of ice water; stir constantly until mixture is spreading consistency. **Yield: 1½ cups.**

Rich Chocolate Frosting:

     1 cup semisweet chocolate morsels
     ½ cup half-and-half
     1 cup butter or margarine
    2½ cups sifted powdered sugar

Combine first 3 ingredients in a saucepan; cook over medium heat, stirring until mixture is smooth. Remove from heat.

Stir in powdered sugar.

Set saucepan in a bowl of ice; beat at medium speed with an electric mixer until frosting holds its shape. **Yield: 3 cups.**

Triple Chocolate Mint-Cream Layer Cake is as delicious as it looks, and the step-by-step photos on the next page show how easy it is to make.

How to Assemble Triple Chocolate Mint-Cream Layer Cake

1. Stack 3 cake layers, rotating each layer until cake is level. Cut a ¼-inch V-shaped notch down one side of cake to use as a guide in assembling a level cake.

2. Slice each cake layer horizontally into 2 layers, using a serrated knife.

3. Place first layer on an 8-inch cardboard round, and spread with one-third of Mint-Cream Filling; top with second layer, lining up notches, and spread with one-half of Chocolate Filling. Top with a third layer, lining up the notches. Repeat layering with remaining Mint-Cream Filling, cake layers, and Chocolate Filling, ending with an unfrosted layer. Wrap and freeze, if desired.

4. To make chocolate-mint triangles, use a sharp knife to cut candies diagonally in half. Dip the blade of the knife into hot water and dry before cutting candies, to eliminate breakage. To make chocolaty-mint shavings, pull a vegetable peeler across the side of candies.

Orange Cheesecake

1½ cups all-purpose flour
⅓ cup sugar
1¼ teaspoons grated orange rind, divided
¾ cup butter or margarine
1 egg yolk, lightly beaten
2 teaspoons orange juice
5 (8-ounce) packages cream cheese, softened
1¾ cups sugar
4 large eggs
¼ cup sour cream
1 teaspoon orange juice
1 cup orange marmalade
1 orange, peeled and sectioned

Combine flour, ⅓ cup sugar, and ¼ teaspoon orange rind; cut in butter with a pastry blender until mixture is crumbly. Add egg yolk and 2 teaspoons orange juice, stirring with a fork until dry ingredients are moistened.

Press mixture on bottom and 2 inches up sides of a 10-inch springform pan. Prick bottom and sides of pastry with a fork.

Bake at 350° for 10 minutes; remove from oven, and set aside.

Beat cream cheese at medium speed with an electric mixer until fluffy. Gradually add 1¾ cups sugar, beating well. Add eggs, 1 at a time, beating after each addition. Stir in sour cream, remaining 1 teaspoon orange rind, and 1 teaspoon orange juice. Pour into prepared pan.

Bake at 350° for 1 hour (center will be soft).

Remove from oven, and run a knife around edge of pan to release sides. Return to oven; turn oven off, and partially open door. Leave cheesecake in oven 30 minutes.

Remove from oven, and cool completely on a wire rack.

Cover, and chill 8 hours.

Melt marmalade in a saucepan over low heat; cool. Spoon over cheesecake, and arrange orange sections on top. **Yield: 10 to 12 servings.**

Sacher Torte

This is the specialty of the house at the famous Hotel Sacher in Vienna.

¾ cup butter or margarine, softened
¾ cup sugar
5 large eggs, separated
4 (1-ounce) squares semisweet chocolate, melted
¾ cup all-purpose flour
½ cup apricot preserves
Chocolate-Honey Glaze

Beat butter at medium speed with an electric mixer until creamy; gradually add sugar, beating well. Add egg yolks, one at a time, beating after each addition. Stir in chocolate. Gradually stir in flour.

Beat egg whites at high speed with an electric mixer until stiff peaks form. Fold one-third of egg whites into chocolate mixture. Fold in remaining egg whites. Spoon into greased and floured 9-inch springform pan or round cakepan.

Bake at 325° for 50 minutes or until a wooden pick inserted in center comes out clean.

Cool in pan on a wire rack 10 minutes. Remove cake from pan, and cool on a wire rack.

Split cake horizontally into 2 layers; set aside.

Heat apricot preserves in small saucepan over low heat; press through a wire-mesh strainer, discarding solids.

Spread preserves between layers.

Pour Chocolate-Honey Glaze over top and sides of cake. **Yield: 1 (9-inch) cake.**

Chocolate-Honey Glaze:

2 (1-ounce) squares unsweetened chocolate
2 (1-ounce) squares semisweet chocolate
1 tablespoon honey
¼ cup butter

Combine all ingredients in a small saucepan; cook, stirring constantly, over low heat until chocolate melts. Cool to room temperature or until slightly thickened.

Bread Plays a Starring Roll

From spicy loaves to sweet coffee cakes, here's just the thing for your bread basket.

Chocolate-Filled Coffee Ring

      1 package active dry yeast
    ¼ cup warm water (105° to 115°)
    ¾ cup milk
    ⅓ cup butter or margarine, cut into chunks
    ¼ cup sugar
      1 teaspoon salt
      2 large eggs, beaten
      1 teaspoon vanilla extract
   3½ to 4 cups all-purpose flour
      1 (6-ounce) package semisweet chocolate
         morsels
    ½ cup chopped pecans
      1 large egg, lightly beaten
      2 cups sifted powdered sugar
   2½ to 3 tablespoons milk

Combine yeast and warm water in a 1-cup liquid measuring cup; let stand 5 minutes.

Combine milk and next 3 ingredients in a saucepan; heat until butter melts, stirring occasionally. Cool to 105° to 115°.

Combine yeast mixture, milk mixture, 2 eggs, and vanilla in a large bowl. Stir in enough flour to make a soft dough.

Turn dough out onto a well-floured surface, and knead until smooth and elastic (about 8 minutes). Place in a well-greased bowl, turning to grease top. Cover and let rise in a warm place (85°), free from drafts, 1½ hours or until doubled in bulk.

Punch dough down; turn out onto a lightly floured surface, and knead 4 or 5 times. Roll into a 22- x 14-inch rectangle; sprinkle evenly with chocolate morsels and nuts, leaving a 1-inch border.

Roll up, jellyroll fashion, starting at long side; moisten edge with water and pinch seam to seal. Place roll, seam side down, on a large greased baking sheet; shape into a ring. Moisten ends with water and pinch together to seal.

Cut dough at 1-inch intervals around ring using a sharp knife or kitchen shears, cutting two-thirds of the way through. Gently turn each piece of dough on its side, slightly overlapping slices.

Cover and let rise in a warm place (85°), free from drafts, 1 hour or until doubled in bulk. Gently brush ring with 1 egg.

Bake at 350° for 25 to 30 minutes or until golden brown. Remove to a wire rack; cool 10 to 15 minutes. (Chocolate-Filled Coffee Ring may be frozen at this point. Wrap ring in foil, omitting glaze, and place in an airtight container. Freeze up to 3 months. Thaw and heat in aluminum foil at 350° for 15 to 20 minutes; drizzle with glaze as directed below.)

Combine powdered sugar and milk; drizzle over warm ring. **Yield: 1 coffee cake.**

Note: 1 (16-ounce) package hot roll mix, prepared according to package directions with 2 tablespoons sugar added, may be substituted for dough. Roll out and proceed as directed.

You can make Chocolate-Filled Coffee Ring ahead of time and freeze it – on Christmas morning, warm up the bread and drizzle on the glaze for a tasty treat.

Upside-Down Cranberry-Apple Coffee Cake

  1 cup fresh or frozen cranberries, thawed
  1 cup finely chopped, unpeeled apple
  ½ cup sugar
  ½ cup chopped walnuts
  ½ teaspoon ground cinnamon
  ⅛ teaspoon ground cloves
  1 cup all-purpose flour
  1 cup sugar
  ¼ cup butter or margarine, melted
  ¼ cup vegetable oil
  2 large eggs
  1 teaspoon vanilla extract

Combine first 6 ingredients; spoon into a greased 8-inch round cakepan; set aside.

Combine flour and remaining ingredients in a mixing bowl; beat at medium speed with an electric mixer 2 minutes. Spoon over cranberry mixture.

Bake at 350° for 55 minutes or until a wooden pick inserted in center comes out clean. Cool in pan on a wire rack 5 minutes; remove from pan. Serve warm, if desired. **Yield: 1 (8-inch) coffee cake.**

Easy Peach Strudel

This was a Test Kitchens favorite – the pastry is delightfully tender!

  1¼ cups all-purpose flour
  ½ cup sour cream
  ½ cup butter or margarine, softened
  1 (12-ounce) jar peach preserves
  ½ cup flaked coconut
  ¼ cup finely chopped walnuts or pecans
    Powdered sugar

Combine first 3 ingredients in a mixing bowl; beat at medium speed with an electric mixer until blended. Shape into a ball; cover with plastic wrap.

Refrigerate at least 1 hour.

Divide dough in half. Roll 1 portion into a 13- x 6-inch rectangle on a well-floured surface. Spread half of preserves over dough, leaving a ½-inch border. Sprinkle with half of coconut and walnuts. Roll up, jellyroll fashion,

starting at long side; pinch seam and ends to seal. Repeat procedure.

Place rolls, seam side down, 3 inches apart on a large baking sheet.

Bake at 450° for 18 to 20 minutes. Remove to a wire rack to cool. Sprinkle with powdered sugar; cut each roll diagonally into 10 slices. **Yield: 20 servings.**

Caramel-Pecan Pinwheels

  ½ cup commercial caramel ice cream topping
  2 tablespoons butter or margarine, melted
  ½ cup chopped pecans
  1 (11-ounce) can refrigerated soft breadsticks

Combine caramel topping and butter; pour into a lightly greased 9-inch square pan. Sprinkle with pecans.

Separate breadsticks, but do not uncoil; place on caramel mixture.

Bake at 350° for 20 to 25 minutes or until golden brown. Remove from oven; let stand 3 minutes.

Invert onto a serving platter; let stand 2 minutes. Remove pan, and serve immediately. **Yield: 8 servings.**

Orange-Butter Rolls

  1 package active dry yeast
  ¼ cup warm water (105° to 115°)
  ½ cup sugar, divided
  2¾ cups all-purpose flour, divided
  ½ cup butter or margarine, melted and divided
  2 large eggs
  ½ cup sour cream
  1 teaspoon salt
  1 cup flaked coconut, divided
  2 tablespoons orange juice
    Orange Glaze

Combine yeast and warm water in a 1-cup liquid measuring cup; let stand 5 minutes.

Combine yeast mixture, ¼ cup sugar, 1 cup flour, 6 tablespoons butter, eggs, sour cream, and salt in a large mixing bowl; beat at medium speed with an electric mixer until well blended. Gradually stir in enough remaining flour to make a stiff dough.

Turn dough out onto a floured surface, and knead 15 times; divide in half.

Roll each portion into a 12-inch circle. Brush with remaining melted butter.

Combine remaining ¼ cup sugar, ¾ cup coconut, and orange juice; sprinkle evenly over circles. Cut each circle into 12 wedges; roll up wedges, beginning at wide end. Place, point side down, into 2 lightly greased 8-inch round cakepans.

Cover and let rise in a warm place (85°), free from drafts, 1 hour and 20 minutes.

Bake at 350° for 20 to 25 minutes or until golden brown. Drizzle with Orange Glaze, and sprinkle with remaining coconut. **Yield: 2 dozen.**

Orange Glaze:

½ cup sugar
⅓ cup sour cream
1½ tablespoons orange juice
2½ tablespoons butter or margarine

Combine all ingredients in a small saucepan; bring to a boil over medium heat, stirring occasionally. Reduce heat, and simmer 3 minutes. **Yield: ¾ cup.**

Eggnog Pancakes

1⅓ cups all-purpose flour
1 teaspoon baking soda
½ teaspoon salt
¼ teaspoon ground nutmeg
⅛ teaspoon ground cloves
¼ cup sugar
1½ cups commercial refrigerated eggnog
1 large egg
1 tablespoon vegetable oil

Combine first 6 ingredients in a bowl; set aside.

Combine eggnog, egg, and oil; stir into dry ingredients, stirring just until moistened.

Pour ¼ cup batter for each pancake onto a hot, lightly greased griddle. Cook until top is covered with bubbles and edges look cooked; turn and cook other side. Serve with butter and powdered sugar, if desired. **Yield: 12 (4-inch) pancakes.**

Note: Eggnog Pancakes may be frozen. Stack pancakes between sheets of wax paper; place in an airtight container. Freeze up to 1 month.

Fruit-and-Nut Bread

1 orange
Boiling water
1 cup raisins
½ cup chopped pecans
1 large egg, lightly beaten
1 cup sugar
2 cups all-purpose flour
1 teaspoon baking powder
½ teaspoon baking soda
½ teaspoon salt

Peel orange; remove white membrane from peel. Set peel aside.

Squeeze orange, reserving juice. Add enough boiling water to juice to measure 1 cup; set aside. Position knife blade in food processor bowl; add orange peel, raisins, and pecans. Process 1 minute, stopping once to scrape sides.

Combine egg and sugar in a large bowl; stir in raisin mixture and orange juice mixture. Add flour and remaining ingredients, stirring just until moistened. Spoon batter into a greased and floured 9- x 5- x 3-inch loafpan.

Bake at 350° for 50 to 55 minutes or until a wooden pick inserted in center comes out clean. Cool in pan on a wire rack 10 minutes; remove from pan, and cool on a wire rack. **Yield: 1 loaf.**

Bread Tips

- Yeast breads are done when an instant-read thermometer placed in center of bread registers 190°.

- Quick breads and yeast breads may be frozen up to 3 months.

- For a warm place for yeast breads to rise, put dough, covered, in a cold oven with a pan of hot water on the rack below.

- To prevent muffins from sticking to paper liners, spray liners with cooking spray before filling.

Overnight Potato Rolls

These rolls are a Test Kitchens favorite because they are unusually light. To make them ahead and freeze them, bake them for 3 to 5 minutes, then wrap in foil and freeze. To serve, let them thaw and then bake at 425° for 5 minutes or until brown.

    1 package active dry yeast
    ½ cup warm water (105° to 115°)
    1 cup skim milk
    ⅔ cup butter-flavored shortening
    ½ cup sugar
  1½ teaspoons salt
    1 cup instant mashed potatoes, prepared
        without salt or fat
    2 large eggs
5¾ to 6¼ cups all-purpose flour
    Melted butter or margarine

Combine yeast and warm water in a 1-cup liquid measuring cup; let stand 5 minutes.

Combine milk and next 4 ingredients in a medium saucepan; cook, stirring constantly, until shortening melts. Cool to 105° to 115°.

Combine yeast mixture, milk mixture, and eggs in a large mixing bowl. Gradually add 3 cups flour, beating at medium speed with an electric mixer until smooth. Stir in enough remaining flour to make a soft dough. Place in a well-greased bowl, turning to grease top; cover.

Refrigerate 8 hours.

Punch dough down; turn out onto a floured surface, and knead 4 or 5 times. Roll dough to ½-inch thickness; cut with a 2½-inch round cutter.

Dip rolls in butter, and place 1 inch apart on lightly greased baking sheets. Cover and let rise in a warm place (85°), free from drafts, 2 hours.

Bake at 425° for 8 to 10 minutes or until lightly browned. **Yield: 2½ dozen.**

Note: To make cloverleaf rolls, shape dough into ¾-inch balls; place 3 balls in each well-greased muffin cup. Proceed as directed.

Jalapeño Parmesan Bread

    1 package active dry yeast
    ½ cup warm water (105° to 115°)
3 to 3½ cups bread flour
    ⅓ cup grated Parmesan cheese
    1 tablespoon sugar
    ½ teaspoon salt
    ½ teaspoon garlic powder
    ¼ teaspoon dried basil
    ¼ teaspoon dried oregano
    ¼ teaspoon crushed red pepper
    ¼ teaspoon dried thyme
    ¼ teaspoon fennel seeds
    1 cup warm water (105° to 115°)
    1 tablespoon olive oil
    ¼ cup pickled jalapeño pepper slices, drained
        and finely chopped
    2 tablespoons grated carrot

Combine yeast and ½ cup warm water in a 1-cup liquid measuring cup; let stand 5 minutes.

Combine flour and next 9 ingredients in a large mixing bowl; make a well in center of mixture. Add yeast mixture, 1 cup water, and olive oil, stirring just until moistened. Stir in jalapeño peppers and carrots.

Turn dough out onto a well-floured surface, and knead 5 minutes. Place in a greased bowl, turning to grease top. Cover and let rise in a warm place (85°), free from drafts, 45 minutes or until doubled in bulk.

Punch dough down, and divide in half. Shape each portion into a loaf, and place in 2 well-greased 8½- x 4½- x 3-inch loafpans. Cover and let rise in a warm place (85°), free from drafts, 30 minutes or until doubled in bulk.

Bake at 350° for 40 to 45 minutes or until loaves sound hollow when tapped. Remove from pans immediately; cool on wire racks. **Yield: 2 loaves.**

Note: For smaller loaves, divide dough into fourths. Shape each portion into a loaf, and place in 4 well-greased 6- x 3½- x 2-inch loafpans. Cover and let rise in a warm place (85°), free from drafts, 30 minutes. Bake at 350° for 30 minutes.

With Date-Nut Bran Muffins, you can have hearty homemade muffins in minutes: start with a mix and add your own dates and pecans.

Date-Nut Bran Muffins

  1 (7-ounce) package bran muffin mix
½ cup chopped dates
½ cup coarsely chopped pecans
  1 tablespoon brown sugar
    Dash of ground cinnamon
  1 large egg
½ cup milk

Combine first 5 ingredients in a large bowl; make a well in center of mixture. Set aside.

Combine egg and milk; add to dry ingredients, stirring just until moistened.

Spoon into greased or paper-lined muffin pans, filling three-fourths full.

Bake at 425° for 12 minutes or until golden. Remove from pans immediately. **Yield: 9 muffins.**

Note: Muffins may be frozen up to 3 months.

Sweet Treats to Share

You can't have too many cookies and or too much candy for the holidays.

Choco-Nut Dainties

 1 cup butter or margarine, softened and divided
 ¾ cup sugar
 1 large egg
 1½ teaspoons vanilla extract
 2¼ cups all-purpose flour
 ½ teaspoon salt
 2 cups (12 ounces) semisweet chocolate
   mini-morsels, divided
 1 cup finely chopped walnuts

Beat ¾ cup butter at medium speed with an electric mixer until creamy; gradually add sugar. Add egg and vanilla, mixing well.

Combine flour and salt; add to butter mixture, mixing until blended. Stir in 1 cup chocolate morsels.

Shape dough into 1½- x ½-inch logs. Place on ungreased cookie sheets.

Bake at 350° for 12 to 15 minutes or until set. Remove to wire racks to cool.

Combine remaining 1 cup chocolate morsels and remaining ¼ cup butter in a small heavy saucepan; cook over low heat, stirring often, until chocolate melts. Dip ends of cookies into mixture, and roll in chopped walnuts. Place on wax paper until chocolate is firm. Store in an airtight container; freeze up to 6 months, if desired. **Yield: 5 dozen.**

Coconut Chews

 ¾ cup butter or margarine, softened
 ¾ cup sifted powdered sugar
 1½ cups all-purpose flour
 2 large eggs
 1 cup firmly packed brown sugar
 2 tablespoons all-purpose flour
 ½ teaspoon baking powder
 ½ teaspoon salt
 ½ teaspoon vanilla extract
 ½ cup chopped pecans
 ½ cup flaked coconut
 1 cup sifted powdered sugar
 2 tablespoons butter or margarine, melted
 3 tablespoons orange juice
 1 teaspoon lemon juice

Beat ¾ cup butter at medium speed with an electric mixer until creamy; gradually add ¾ cup powdered sugar and 1½ cups flour, beating well. Press into an ungreased 13- x 9- x 2-inch pan.

Bake at 350° for 12 minutes.

Combine eggs and next 7 ingredients; pour evenly over crust.

Bake at 350° for 20 minutes.

Combine 1 cup powdered sugar and remaining ingredients, stirring until smooth. Pour over warm cookies. Cool completely on a wire rack. Cut into 3- x 1-inch bars. Freeze up to 3 months, if desired. **Yield: 3 dozen.**

Wrap up an assortment of cookies and candies for teachers, friends, and neighbors, and keep some on hand to serve when friends drop by: clockwise from top, Choco-Nut Dainties, Coconut Chews, and Toasted Almond Confections.

Toasted Almond Confections

1 (7-ounce) jar marshmallow cream
1 (1-pound) package powdered sugar, sifted
1 tablespoon milk
¼ teaspoon almond extract
1 (14-ounce) package caramels, unwrapped
2 tablespoons water
1½ to 2 cups chopped almonds, toasted

Combine first 4 ingredients in a large mixing bowl; beat at low speed with an electric mixer until well blended, stopping often to scrape sides of bowl. (Mixture will be dry.)

Divide mixture into 4 portions. Shape each portion into a 6-inch log. Wrap in plastic wrap, and chill 2 to 3 hours.

Combine caramels and water in top of a double boiler; bring water to a boil. Reduce heat to low; cook until caramels melt, stirring often.

Unwrap each log; dip in caramel, and roll in almonds. Wrap in wax paper or aluminum foil; chill 1 hour. Cut into ¼-inch slices to serve. (Wrapped, uncut logs can be stored in refrigerator or frozen up to 1 month.) **Yield: 4 (6-inch) logs.**

Cherry Surprise Balls

¾ cup butter or margarine, softened
½ cup sifted powdered sugar
2 cups sifted cake flour
1 teaspoon vanilla extract
½ cup chopped pecans
14 red or green candied cherries, cut in half
   Powdered sugar

Beat butter at medium speed with an electric mixer until creamy; gradually add powdered sugar, beating well. Gradually add flour, beating until blended. Stir in vanilla and pecans. Cover and chill 1 hour.

Shape dough around each cherry half to form a ¾-inch ball. Place balls 2 inches apart on ungreased cookie sheets.

Bake at 375° for 20 minutes. Roll in powdered sugar while warm. Cool on wire racks. **Yield: 28 cookies.**

Christmas Pinwheel Cookies

½ cup shortening
¾ cup sugar
1 large egg
1 tablespoon milk
1 teaspoon vanilla extract
1¼ cups all-purpose flour
½ teaspoon baking powder
¼ teaspoon salt
½ cup chopped walnuts
¼ cup chopped red candied cherries
¼ cup chopped green candied cherries

Beat shortening at medium speed with an electric mixer until fluffy; gradually add sugar, beating well. Add egg, milk, and vanilla, mixing well.

Combine flour, baking powder, and salt; gradually add to shortening mixture, mixing well. Cover dough, and chill 8 hours or until firm.

Position knife blade in food processor bowl; add walnuts and cherries. Pulse 6 to 8 times or until finely chopped.

Roll dough to a 10-inch square on a heavily floured surface. Sprinkle with fruit mixture; roll dough, jellyroll fashion. Wrap in wax paper; chill 8 hours or freeze until firm enough to slice.

Cut log into ¼-inch slices, and place on greased cookie sheets.

Bake at 400° for 10 to 12 minutes. Remove to wire racks to cool. **Yield: 3 dozen.**

Almond-Caramel Bars

1¾ cups all-purpose flour
½ cup sugar
2 teaspoons baking powder
¼ teaspoon salt
½ cup butter or margarine, softened
1 large egg
½ cup butter or margarine
¼ cup sugar
3 tablespoons honey
2 tablespoons milk
2 (2¼-ounce) packages sliced almonds
1 teaspoon almond extract

Combine first 4 ingredients; cut in ½ cup butter with pastry blender until mixture is crumbly. Add egg, stirring until blended. (Mixture will be crumbly.) Press mixture evenly into a 15- x 10- x 1-inch jellyroll pan, and prick with a fork.

Bake at 350° for 5 minutes.

Combine ½ cup butter and next 4 ingredients in a heavy saucepan. Bring to a boil over medium heat; boil 1 minute. Let cool.

Stir in almond extract, and pour over crust.

Bake at 350° for 20 minutes or until golden brown. Cool 10 minutes on a wire rack. Cut into bars, and cool completely. Store in an airtight container. **Yield: 4 dozen.**

Oatmeal Cookies

   1 cup shortening
   1 cup sugar
   1 cup firmly packed brown sugar
   2 large eggs
   1 tablespoon vanilla extract
1⅔ cups all-purpose flour
   1 teaspoon baking soda
 ½ teaspoon salt
   1 teaspoon ground cinnamon
   1 teaspoon ground ginger
   3 cups quick-cooking oats, uncooked
   1 cup chopped pecans
   1 cup raisins

Beat shortening at medium speed with an electric mixer until fluffy; gradually add sugars, beating well. Add eggs and vanilla, mixing well.

Combine flour and next 4 ingredients; add to shortening mixture, mixing until blended. Stir in remaining ingredients.

Drop dough by tablespoonfuls onto lightly greased cookie sheets.

Bake at 350° for 10 minutes or until lightly browned. Remove to wire racks to cool. **Yield: 5 dozen.**

Chocolate-Almond Bites

   6 (1-ounce) squares semisweet chocolate
 ⅓ cup unsalted butter
   2 large eggs, lightly beaten
 ½ cup all-purpose flour
 ½ cup sugar
 ½ teaspoon baking powder
   1 teaspoon vanilla extract
   1 cup chopped almonds
     Velvet Chocolate Frosting
     Chopped almonds

Combine chocolate and butter in a heavy saucepan; cook over low heat, stirring often, until chocolate melts. Remove from heat; gradually stir in eggs.

Combine flour, sugar, and baking powder; gradually stir into chocolate mixture. Stir in vanilla and 1 cup almonds. Spoon into lined miniature (1¾-inch) muffin pans, filling two-thirds full.

Bake at 350° for 8 minutes (tops will be slightly soft). Remove from pans; cool on wire racks.

Spread with Velvet Chocolate Frosting; sprinkle with chopped almonds. Store in refrigerator or freeze up to 2 weeks. **Yield: 5 dozen.**

Velvet Chocolate Frosting:

 ½ cup whipping cream
 ¾ cup sugar
   3 (1-ounce) squares unsweetened chocolate
   1 egg yolk, lightly beaten
   2 tablespoons butter or margarine, softened
   1 teaspoon vanilla extract

Combine whipping cream and sugar in a small heavy saucepan; bring to a boil over medium heat, stirring constantly. Reduce heat, and simmer 5 minutes, stirring often.

Add chocolate, and cook, stirring constantly, until chocolate melts.

Stir about one-fourth of hot mixture into egg yolk; return to remaining hot mixture, and cook 30 seconds, stirring constantly. Remove from heat. Stir in butter and vanilla. **Yield: 1⅓ cups.**

Shortbread Cookies

⅓ cup butter, softened
¼ cup sugar
2 teaspoons cognac or brandy
1 cup all-purpose flour
⅛ teaspoon salt
   Sugar

Position knife blade in food processor bowl; add butter and sugar, and pulse 5 times. Sprinkle with cognac, and add flour and salt.

Process 30 seconds or until well blended, stopping once to scrape sides of bowl.

Shape dough into ¾-inch balls, and place on ungreased cookie sheets. Dip a cookie stamp or the bottom of a glass in sugar and flatten each ball.

Bake at 350° for 12 to 18 minutes or until edges begin to brown. Remove to wire racks to cool. **Yield: 2 dozen.**

Creamy Pralines

2½ cups sugar
1 cup buttermilk
1 teaspoon baking soda
1 tablespoon butter or margarine
1 teaspoon vanilla extract
2 cups pecan halves
   Vegetable cooking spray

Combine first 3 ingredients in a heavy 4-quart saucepan.

Bring to a boil over medium heat, stirring often; reduce heat to low, and cook, stirring occasionally, until a candy thermometer reaches 236° (about 25 minutes).

Remove from heat; stir in butter, and let mixture cool to 140° (about 30 minutes).

Add vanilla, beating until color lightens; stir in pecans. Working rapidly, drop by tablespoonfuls onto wax paper coated with cooking spray; let stand until firm. **Yield: 2 dozen.**

Espresso-and-Cream Brownies

2 (1-ounce) squares unsweetened chocolate
½ cup butter or margarine
2 to 3 teaspoons instant coffee granules
1¼ cups sugar, divided
⅛ teaspoon salt
3 large eggs, divided
⅓ cup all-purpose flour
1 (8-ounce) package cream cheese, softened
½ teaspoon vanilla extract

Combine first 3 ingredients in a large heavy saucepan; cook over low heat, stirring occasionally, until chocolate melts. Remove from heat.

Add ¾ cup sugar and salt to chocolate mixture, stirring until blended. Add 2 eggs, 1 at a time, beating after each addition. Stir in flour. Spread mixture into a greased and floured 9-inch square pan; set aside.

Combine cream cheese, remaining ½ cup sugar, remaining egg, and vanilla in a small bowl; beat at medium speed with an electric mixer until smooth. Drop mixture by tablespoonfuls over chocolate layer, and swirl with a knife.

Bake at 350° for 35 to 40 minutes or until set. Cool on a wire rack. Cut into squares. **Yield: 16 brownies.**

Creamy Peanut Butter Fudge

2 cups sugar
⅔ cup milk
2 tablespoons light corn syrup
½ cup chunky peanut butter
1 teaspoon vanilla extract

Combine first 3 ingredients in a large saucepan. Bring to a boil over medium heat, stirring constantly.

Cook, stirring occasionally, until mixture reaches soft ball stage or a candy thermometer reaches 240°. Remove from heat.

Add peanut butter and vanilla, beating 5 to 7 minutes or until mixture is creamy.

Spoon into a buttered 8-inch square pan, and spread evenly; cool. Cut into squares, and store in an airtight container. **Yield: 1¼ pounds.**

Chocolate Biscotti is baked twice – once as a log and again after slicing. Eat it the Italian way – by dipping it into a cup of steaming hot coffee before taking a bite!

Chocolate Biscotti

    4 (1-ounce) squares unsweetened
        chocolate
 ½ cup butter or margarine
 ½ teaspoon vanilla extract
    3 large eggs
1¼ cups sugar
    3 cups all-purpose flour
 ½ teaspoon baking powder
    1 cup walnuts or hazelnuts, chopped
    1 egg white, lightly beaten

Melt chocolate and butter in a heavy saucepan over low heat; remove from heat. Stir in vanilla; cool.

Beat eggs at medium speed with an electric mixer until frothy; gradually add sugar, beating until thick and pale (about 5 minutes). Add chocolate mixture, stirring until blended.

Combine flour and baking powder; stir into chocolate mixture. Stir in nuts.

Flour hands, and form dough into a 13-inch log. Place on a lightly greased baking sheet. Brush with egg white.

Bake at 350° for 45 minutes; cool on a wire rack.

Cut log with a serrated knife crosswise into 24 (½-inch) slices, and place on an ungreased cookie sheet.

Bake at 350° for 10 minutes on each side. Remove to wire racks to cool. **Yield: 2 dozen.**

Creamy Coffee Punch is made with two flavors of ice cream and spiked with Kahlúa and brandy.

Drinks All Around

Fix sippers for two or punch for a crowd; there's a recipe here to fit the occasion.

Coffee Punch

- ¾ cup ground coffee
- 2 quarts water
- 2 cups coffee ice cream, softened
- 1 cup vanilla ice cream, softened
- ½ cup Kahlúa or other coffee-flavored liqueur
- ½ cup brandy
- ⅓ cup sugar (optional)
- 2 cups coffee ice cream
- 1 cup vanilla ice cream
- 1 cup whipping cream
- 2 tablespoons powdered sugar
  Ground cinnamon

Prepare coffee according to manufacturer's directions using ¾ cup ground coffee and 2 quarts water. Cool.

Combine coffee, 2 cups coffee ice cream, 1 cup vanilla ice cream, liqueurs, and, if desired, sugar in a large bowl; beat at medium speed with a portable electric mixer until smooth. Pour into a punch bowl.

Scoop 2 cups coffee ice cream and 1 cup vanilla ice cream into coffee mixture.

Combine whipping cream and powdered sugar; beat at medium speed with an electric mixer until soft peaks form. Dollop over coffee mixture; sprinkle with cinnamon.
Yield: about 3½ quarts.

Sherried Fruit Drink

2 cups grape juice, chilled
1 cup pineapple juice, chilled
1 cup orange juice, chilled
1 cup dry sherry

Combine all ingredients; serve immediately. **Yield: 5 cups.**

Hot Pineapple-Cranberry Punch

2¼ cups unsweetened pineapple juice
2 cups cranberry juice cocktail
1½ cups water
2 tablespoons brown sugar
3 (2-inch) sticks cinnamon
1 tablespoon whole cloves
1½ teaspoons whole allspice

Combine first 3 ingredients in a 10- to 12-cup electric percolator. Place brown sugar and remaining ingredients in percolator basket.

Perk through complete cycle. Serve hot. **Yield: 6 cups.**

Note: For a party, triple recipe, and perk in a 30-cup party percolator.

Fireside Chocolate

4 cups milk
5 (1-ounce) squares semisweet chocolate, chopped
2 (3-inch) sticks cinnamon
1 teaspoon vanilla extract
Whipped cream (optional)
Ground cinnamon (optional)

Combine first 4 ingredients in a large saucepan; cook over medium heat, stirring constantly, until chocolate melts and mixture is hot. Remove from heat. Remove and discard cinnamon sticks.

Beat mixture at high speed with an electric mixer 1 to 2 minutes. Pour into mugs; if desired, dollop with whipped cream and sprinkle with cinnamon. Serve immediately. **Yield: 4½ cups.**

Mint Velvet

1 cup vanilla ice cream
¼ cup Vandermint liqueur or other chocolate-mint flavored liqueur
¼ cup half-and-half
2 teaspoons instant decaffeinated coffee granules

Combine all ingredients in container of an electric blender; process until smooth. Serve immediately. **Yield: 1½ cups.**

Whispers

1 pint coffee ice cream
½ cup brandy
½ cup white crème de cacao
2 tablespoons milk

Combine all ingredients in container of an electric blender; process until smooth. Serve immediately. **Yield: 3¼ cups.**

Spiced Apple Punch

1 gallon apple juice
1 (750-milliliter) bottle rum
1 lemon slice
1 orange slice
6 whole cloves
3 (2-inch) sticks cinnamon

Pour apple juice and rum into a 30-cup electric percolator. Place lemon slice and remaining ingredients in percolator basket.

Perk through complete cycle. Serve hot. **Yield: 5 quarts.**

General Index

Recipe Index

A listing of every recipe by food category and/or major ingredient

Alma Lynne Angel

Instructions are on page 88.

Dimensions for Duplicate Stitch
sweater gauge 6 x 8
design area 13" x 18"
Duplicate stitch with checkerboard

Dimensions for Cross-Stitch

Fabric Count	Design Area	Cutting Dimensions
22	3⅛" x 6"	9⅛" x 12"
18	3⅞" x 7¼"	9⅞" x 13¼"
14	5" x 9⅜"	11" x 15⅜"
25 (over 2)	5½" x 10½"	11½" x 16½"
11	6⅜" x 11⅞"	12⅜" x 17⅞"

Cross-stitch without checkerboard

How to Duplicate-Stitch

Each square on graph represents 1 duplicate stitch. Thread tapestry needle with floss and bring up through fabric from back to front at A. Insert needle at B and pull floss through. Bring needle back through A to wrong side. Repeat to complete row, working from right to left. If vertical stitches are required, stitch from top to bottom.

Block design by pressing on wrong side with pressing cloth and steam iron. To launder, hand-wash and lay flat to dry.

Color Key

Step 1: Duplicate stitch (6 strands)
Cross-stitch (2 strands)
(*Note:* Numbers are for DMC floss. The number in parentheses indicates whole skeins used for duplicate stitch on sweater.)

	(1) White
221	(1) Very Dark Shell Pink
223	(3) Medium Shell Pink
224	(3) Light Shell Pink
326	(1) Very Dark Rose
353	(1) Peach
436	(1) Tan
437	(1) Light Tan
500	(1) Very Dark Blue Green
501	(1) Dark Blue Green
502	(2) Blue Green
754	(1) Light Peach
798	(1) Dark Delft
823	(5) Dark Navy Blue
899	(1) Medium Rose
948	(1) Very Light Peach
3721	(1) Dark Shell Pink
002	(1) Balger HL Gold

Step 2: Backstitch (2 strands)

326 Very Dark Rose

For sweater, use 2 *additional* skeins of light tan for braids. For pillow, use 1 *additional* skein for braids.

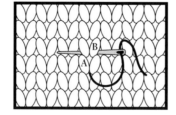

Checkerboard Chart for Duplicate Stitch and Cross-Stitch

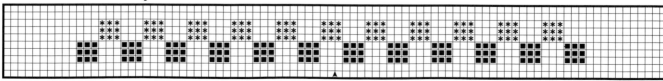

Center

Center

Center

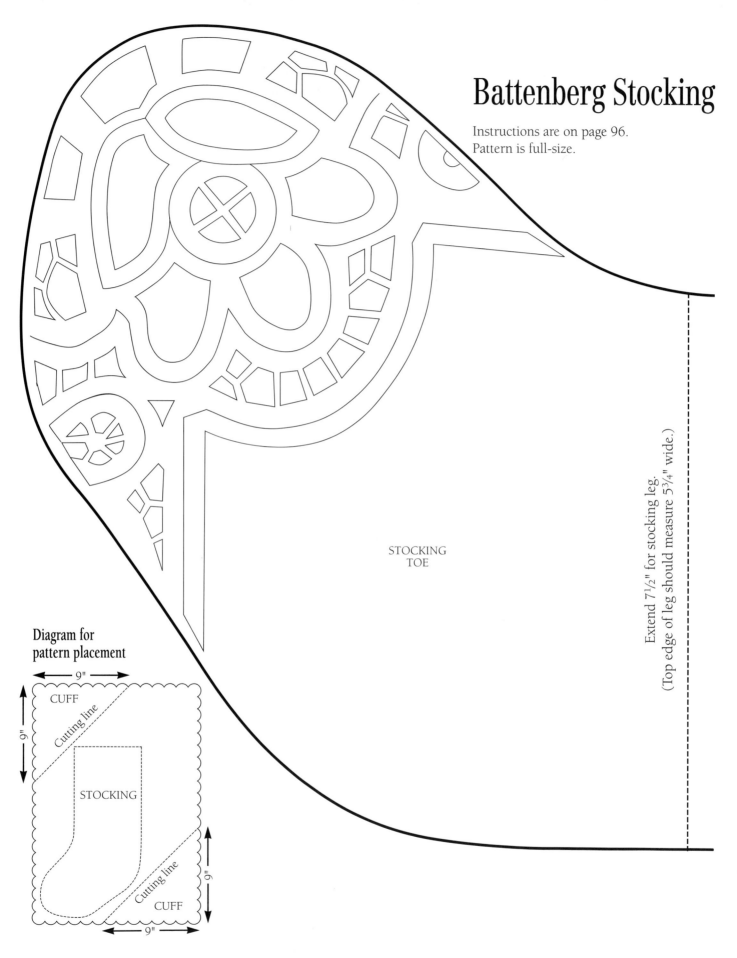

Battenberg Stocking

Instructions are on page 96.
Pattern is full-size.

STOCKING
TOE

Extend 7¹/₂" for stocking leg.
(Top edge of leg should measure 5³/₄" wide.)

Diagram for pattern placement

9"

CUFF

Cutting line

9"

STOCKING

Cutting line

9"

CUFF

9"

Knitted Wreath

Instructions are on page 98.

Knitting Chart

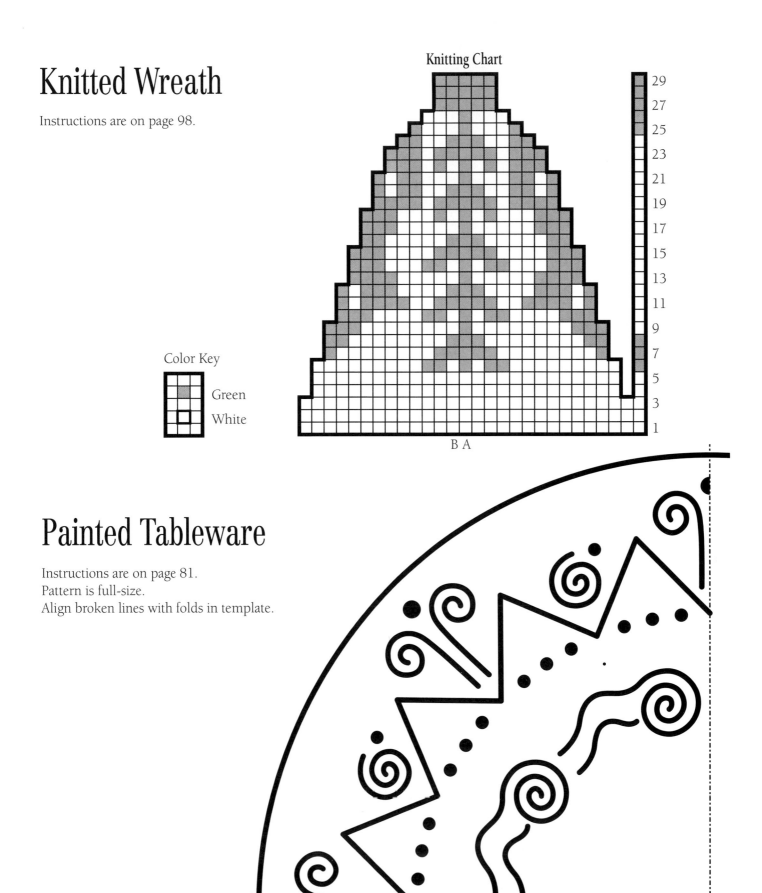

29
27
25
23
21
19
17
15
13
11
9
7
5
3
1

B A

Color Key

Green

White

Painted Tableware

Instructions are on page 81.
Pattern is full-size.
Align broken lines with folds in template.

Pint-size Piñatas

Instructions are on page 101.
Patterns are full-size.

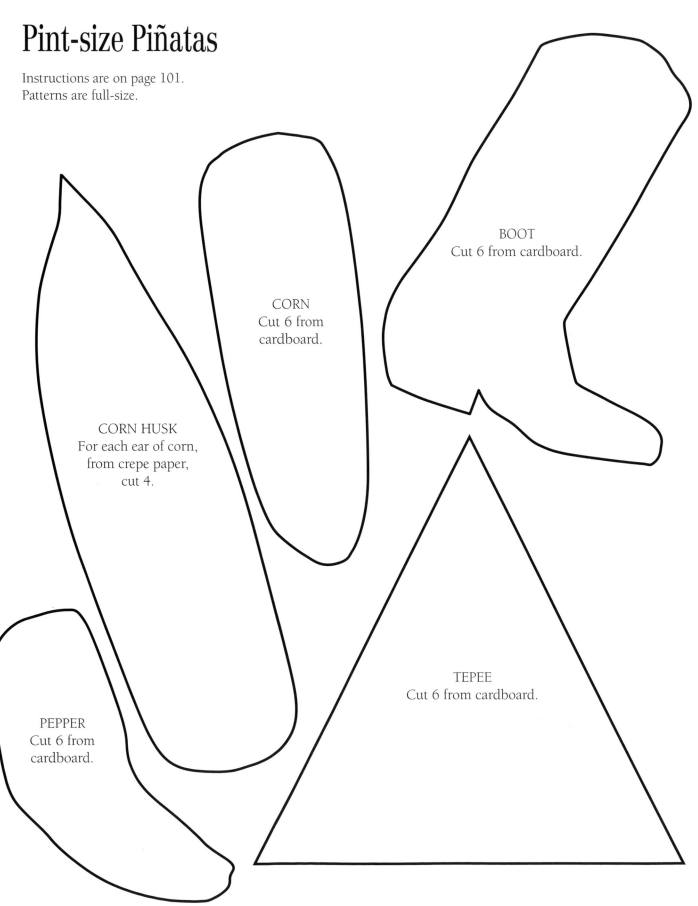

CORN
Cut 6 from
cardboard.

BOOT
Cut 6 from cardboard.

CORN HUSK
For each ear of corn,
from crepe paper,
cut 4.

TEPEE
Cut 6 from cardboard.

PEPPER
Cut 6 from
cardboard.

Twinkle, Twinkle, Ribbon Stars

Instructions are on page 82.
Patterns are full-size.

Diagram
Star points are shown in
diagram from back side.
Place glue at dots.

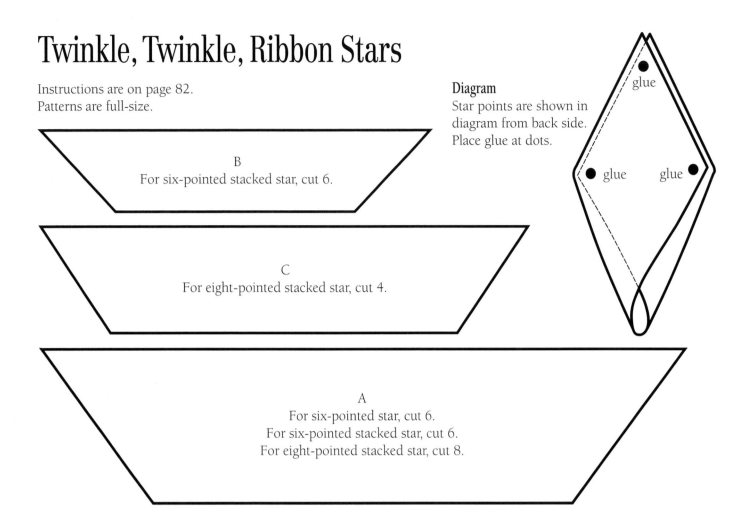

B
For six-pointed stacked star, cut 6.

C
For eight-pointed stacked star, cut 4.

A
For six-pointed star, cut 6.
For six-pointed stacked star, cut 6.
For eight-pointed stacked star, cut 8.

Gift Label

Instructions appear in the
cutline on page 127.
Pattern is full-size.

TO:

FROM:

Contributors

Designers

Becky Dossey and James Preuss, mantel, 60-61; trees, 54-55.

Susan Z. Douglas, knitted wreath, 98-99.

Connie Formby, label, 126-27.

Bob Gager, bottle stoppers,118, 119.

Charlotte Hagood, crocheted cottage, 97; leaf-printed ornaments, 92-93; ribbon stars, 82-83.

Françoise Dudal Kirkman, garden angel, 104-105; painted plate, 80-81.

Dondra Parham, beaded ornaments, 90-91.

Carol S. Richard, pomanders, 84-85.

Katie Stoddard, embellished candles, 56-57.

Evelyn Thompson, folk-art jewelry, 102-103.

Carol M. Tipton, tree skirt and stocking, 94-96.

Photographers

All photographs by John O'Hagan except the following:

Jim Bathie, 64 far right.

Ralph Anderson, 41, 75.

Langdon Clay, 20-23.

Tina Evans, 108-50.

Mary-Gray Hunter, 99.

Gene Johnson, 16-19.

Happy Kozel, 36.

Chris A. Little, 27-29, 32-35, 38-40, 58-59.

Hal Lott, 44-55, 60-61, 73.

Sylvia Martin, 30-31.

Tim Rhoad, 33 top.

Melissa Springer, 86-89.

Photostylists

All photostyling by Katie Stoddard except the following:

Bob Gager, 108-50.

Nancy Ingram, 16-19.

Joetta Moulden, 44-55, 60-61.

Bettie Bearden Pardee, 62-65.

Acknowledgments

Many thanks to the following for their kind assistance:

Laurel Springs Fraser Firs, Laurel Springs, North Carolina

Roy Nicoles, Greenfield Farms, Ridgeland, Mississippi

Sheila Pickles, *Christmas,* © 1989, Harmony Books

The homes featured on pages 50-55 and 60-61 appeared on the Kappa Kappa Gamma Christmas Pilgrimage in Houston, Texas.